The Black Corleones

Part 2: Love Ain't Loyal

Inspired by True Events

Bella Jones

AUG   2015

FR

Published: 2014

TBRS Publications

Copyright © 2014 TBRS Publications

Copyright © 2014 Bella Jones

The Black Corleones

Part 2: Love Ain't Loyal

Inspired by True Events

Word from the Author:

      The characters in this book represent 5 men I've had the pleasure of knowing and going through life with. My experiences with them forever changed and shaped my life. Without their impact on my life, I wouldn't have had the courage to pen this story or any story for that matter. This book is based on true events, but some characters you meet and some scenes you will encounter are embellished and exaggerated to add to the entertainment of the story. Although there is embellishment, The Black Corleones are based on a true story of those five young men I met when I was just a girl. They changed me into the *HUSTLER* I am today. – *Bella Jones.*

Guy told me one time; don't let yourself get attached to anything you're not willing to walk out on in thirty seconds flat if you feel the heat coming from around the corner. Now, if you're around me, you gotta move when I move.

-The Black Corleones 2 Love Ain't Loyal-

Chapter One

With a sinister look on his face, Samir motioned for Carlos to bring him the electrical wires. As he touched the two ends together, he watched the fear in Kyle's face replace the cocky demeanor as the electrical sparks lit up the room.

"Just kill you huh? Naw my nigga, I'm going to inflict the same pain you thought you were inflicting on me when you ran in my spots and took my bread. It's much more gratifying for me and my crew to watch you die a slow death. See, you made the decision to take my shit, so since you like being the nigga that give the orders; I'm going to sit back and watch you kill yourself. I'm gonna watch you inflict pain on yourself until your fucking heart explodes, bitch. You see my nigga, I'm the fucking boss, and I give the fucking orders, so I'm gon' teach you a lesson. But first, I'm gonna take care of your mans' here. Mek, wake this nigga up," Samir said with a devilish grin on his face.

Meko hesitated at first because he was in shock at Samir's reaction. He had never seen this side of an otherwise mild tempered Samir. Frankly, Meko thought he was going to be the one doing the murders and Samir would just be there to make sure it got done. He knew right then that Samir had a killer instinct in him. It just took a threat of destroying what he was trying to build to bring it out of him.

"Say, hoe ass nigga, wake yo' pussy ass up," Meko demanded as he slapped Kyle's partner to wake him.

"Where... where am I?" Kyle's right hand man asked, just as the pain began to set in.

"You're in hell my nigga, and me... I'm Lucifer himself," Samir replied.

"Please man, let me go. I don't want to die like this," the man pleaded

"Let you go, yea, we gon' let you go, right after you tell us where our work and our doe is. We gon' let you go straight to the morgue, Joe," Meko burst out in laughter.

Cesar stood behind the rest of his crew, shocked that his boys had turned into such ruthless niggas in less than 24 hours. He didn't get in the game to kill niggas, he just wanted to make money, but he

2

knew that one day the youngsters would have to get their hands dirty and when he pulled the trigger the night before, his entire demeanor changed. He knew he could kill if he needed. It's easy to put a bullet in a nigga's brain, but the torture game wasn't his forte. He knew he couldn't challenge Samir in this moment because he was the one who introduced them to Kyle in the first place. He couldn't, however, just act as if Samir's dominance as a leader of the crew wasn't fucking with him. He started to think that even though Samir didn't always say he was the boss, his reaction to Cesar over the last month was starting to make him feel as if he was beneath Samir. But for now he would just shake those feeling off and finish the work they were there to do.

"So, tell us homie, before things get real ugly, what did you do with the birds and the money you took from my spot?" Seven asked Kyle as he lit the blow torch.

"I ain't telling you pussy ass Corleones shit, just kill me, fucking kill me!" Kyle responded.

"You might want to reconsider that answer, Joe. See, Seven here is a little vexed right now cuz' he was supposed to be fucking this little Puerto Rican bitch from out west, and you have no idea what a nigga will do with a case of blue balls," Chase laughed as he stood against the basement wall, looking down at his two-way.

"How much you fuck with this nigga hanging next to you? This is your man twenty grand or what, cuz' I'm gon' ask you one more time where we can locate our shit," Seven asked again.

"Fuck you lame niggas, fuck you! Kill me now, nigga!" Kyle yelled.

"Okay then, fine, have it your way," Seven said as he burned portions of his body. He screamed in gut wrenching agony as he tried to move away from the blow torch. His skin began to melt off as if it was wax on a candle. He begged Kyle to tell them what they wanted to hear. Kyle didn't want to show fear to a group of niggas he despised, but watching what they were doing to his friend he grew up with from second grade was too much for him to bare. He closed his eyes and tried to escape the sight of their torture.

Meko gut punched Kyle when he caught his eyes closing. He wanted Kyle to watch every bit of what he was causing.

"Oh no bitch, you got a front row seat to this, and if I catch you closing your eyes again I'm gon' cut your eyelids off, hoe," Meko snapped.

"Sev, that's enough," Samir said grabbing Sevens hand.

"Kyle, just tell us where it is, and this can all be over dude." Cesar said.

"Yea, just tell us," Meko repeated looking at Cesar in disgust.

"Okay, okay, okay, just leave my bro alone. You hoe ass niggas got what you wanted. Just leave my bro out of this," Kyle pleaded.

"Got what we wanted? Bitch, my work and my money is gone. That's what I want; killing you is just a bonus," Samir put the broken electrical wires to Kyle's balls.

"Please, I'll tell you... I'll tell you..." Kyle barely got the words out in the middle of the electrical shock surging through his body.

"Awwww, look at him. This bitch ain't so tuff after all," Chase laughed.

"The work and money is stashed at my spot in Harvey. One eleven thirty two Lexington Ave. Now just kill me, you got what you want."

"We will; after we make sure you ain't bullshitting us," Meko responded.

"Chase, you and Cesar go to Harvey and make sure this nigga ain't lying. Call me the second y'all get there," Samir commanded of his crew.

"I swear to you Joe if my shit ain't where you say it is, I'm gon' send pieces of you to your momma until my money and my work is recovered," Samir promised.

Samir sent Cesar with Chase to recovery their drugs and money because frankly it was all Cesar's fault. His greed made him throw caution out of the window. They were a family and Cesar knew that he could get them to side with him. Samir was beating himself up over it. He knew in the last 48 hours he had to take more of a leadership role opposed to a brotherly one when it came to Cesar. This was business, and he couldn't allow anything to hinder their business. It was their first mishap in the game that Samir realized they had to learn how to separate business from personal issues. He decided that they would keep their voting system, but he would be the one who made the judgment call at the end of the day.

On their ride to Kyle's stash spot, Cesar sat in silence. He was hoping that Kyle wasn't fucking with them so he could regain his dignity in the eyes of his brothers. He knew he fucked up. He knew he should have used his better discretion, but he also thought his brothers were over reacting to the situation. He felt they were making it bigger than it had to be and they joined the game to make money, not torture and kill people.

"Man, this shit is way out of hand. Niggas is really tripping right now behind this. I think we're going a little too far, bro."

"*Too far, nigga what?* We are rookies in this game Ces. We can't let niggas think because we're young we soft out here. Muthafuckers been talking about how we being spoon fed and shit and that this shit we doing is only because Samir is Carlyle's son; we can't have no fucking body robbing us. The city is watching. We supposed to be corner hustling at our age, but instead we boss niggas in this game. So fuck no, we ain't over reacting. Nigga, we sending a message," Chase responded.

"Y'all stay saying the hood is watching and talking, I ain't heard shit about niggas looking down on us. We get love out here."

"That's the problem. You don't hear shit cuz you don't want to hear shit. Get your head out the clouds, bro. This game is not just about the money, Ces. You are so focused on your greed that you allowing yourself to make fucked up decisions. I ain't blaming you for this shit cuz' we made the decision as a team, but you need to accept some responsibility. Niggas want us to fail bro, and you can't even see it."

"I ain't a dumb nigga, Chase. I'm in these streets every day. I'm in the trenches twenty four seven, Joe. So, don't tell me what I don't see or what I'm being blind to, Cesar snapped.

"Oh, yeah, since you out here so tough, how this nigga Kyle planning to fuck us over slip past you, Mr. *I'm in the trenches*? Just own up and be more careful to your fucking surroundings. I ain't get in this game to murk niggas either, but I will if it means protecting The Black Corleones and the name we building for this family. Funny thing is we got it easy cuz' all the pressure falls on Samir. That nigga got mad calls about this shit from all the higher-ups, and he's the one that has to deal with the most bullshit."

"Ain't no use in crying over spilled milk though. That's all I'm saying," Cesar said blowing off the point Chase was trying to make.

"My nigga, you're a lost cause. Slow the fuck down, I think this the spot," Chase interjected. "I hope you strapped and ready to unload on whatever is behind them walls, Ces."

Chase and Cesar walked to the door of the home that Kyle assured their work and money could be located. Chase motioned to Cesar to knock on the door as he stood on the side, out of sight with his .45 in his hand, cocked and ready.

Camille, Kyle's longtime bitch answered the door in nothing but a towel expecting it to be Kyle coming home.

"It's about time, nigga," she said without even

realizing she was about to be ambushed. Her eyes widened when she finally saw the two Corleones standing at her door. She tried to close it quickly, but Chase kicked the door, knocking her to the ground.

"Damn nigga, did you have to be so rough, this bitch is fine as fuck," Cesar said, rubbing his dick as he canvassed Camille's naked body.

"Wake the fuck up Ces, we here for one reason and one reason only. You really pissing me the fuck off, bro; handle your fucking business nigga," Chase snapped. "Bitch, who else is in this fucking house with you?"

"Nobody, I'm here alone," she responded.

"Cesar, check the fucking house while I tie this hoe up."

"The bitch said she's alone," Cesar interjected.

"Check the fucking house Cesar, I swear to my mother this is not a fucking game."

Cesar reluctantly did what Chase told him to do. This entire situation was starting to get under his skin. He was starting to feel like the rest of the crew was treating him like a bitch behind this one situation, and he was by far no bitch made nigga. He said his peace to his crew already, but if niggas still wanted to hold a grudge he would have to show them he was still the same old Ces.

"Where did your man put our shit, Lil' Momma?" Chase continued to integrate Camille.

I don't know what you're talking about," she lied

"Look bitch, I don't have time to play with you. I got your nigga, and he sent me here, so where's my shit?"

"I don't believe you. Kyle is coming here tonight, and when I tell him you Corleone niggas kicked our door in, he's gonna kill you!"

"Oh, is that right. He's going to kill us?" Chase laugh. Just then Cesar returned.

"Ces, this bitch just said the funniest shit. She just informed me that when Kyle catches us, he's gon' kill us," Chase joked.

"Oh, is that so? Say lil' momma, dead niggas can't kill niggas."

Camille still had no clue that Kyle wouldn't make it home that night, so she held her ground. She was a loyal bitch, and she would give her own life to hold Kyle down. Chase sensed that she needed a little incentive, so he gave her one.

"Yo, Meko, are you there?" Chase chirped Meko on his Nextel phone.

"I'm here bro, what's the status, is the stuff there or is this nigga bluffing?" Meko responded.

"We here and I believe it's here, but this nigga's bitch tryna be on some Bonnie and Clyde shit, playing the dumb role. Talking about, when that nigga catch us he murking all of us," Chase laughed hard.

"Oh really, well, that's gon' be hard to do seeing as I got this nigga tied up right now."

Camille's eyes widened when she heard the words come through Chase's speaker. She still kept her game face on because she figured this could just be a ploy to give them what they wanted. She knew if she gave in to their demands, and Kyle was okay, she would have bigger problems when he returned home. She kept her mouth closed until Meko did the unspeakable.

"Well then, let me let this nigga talk to his bitch one last time," Meko chirped back.

Camille's heart drop when she heard Kyle's voice. He was in obvious pain, telling her to give them what they came for. With tears in her eyes, she tried to speak to Kyle, but Chase intervened.

"Bitch, go get my shit and then maybe I'll let you say goodbye." he told her as he pushed her down the hallway.

"This nigga is really dumber than I thought. How you stick niggas up and then stash the shit in your own house?" Cesar inquired.

"The same way we got in bed with that nigga; for money," Chase replied.

Camille returned five minutes later pulling 3 large duffle bags. She dropped them at Cesar's feet and headed back into her bedroom to retrieve the rest. In less than 24 hours, the Corleones recovered all the money and work that was stolen from them. They had rectified the situation before it got any worse.

Chase chirped Meko and Samir on the Nextel and confirmed everything. Then he put a bullet in Camille's head and him and Cesar headed back to the city to join Meko, Samir and Seven.

"Did you get it all back, bro?" Samir asked when Chase and Cesar finally returned to the city.

"I did fam, don't worry about nothing, we good," Chased answered.

"Cool, what you do with his bitch?" Samir asked.

"I sent her on a vacation, forever," Chase smiled.

Samir's mind was finally at ease. He knew he had to come strong to fix the predicament they found themselves in. He could finally rest knowing he had sent a message across Chicago that although they were young, they were not to be fucked with.

He looked Kyle in his eyes one last time. The fact that Kyle threatened his legacy so early in the game infuriated Samir to his core. He commissioned Meko to end his partner's life.

"What you want me to do with this nigga here?"

Meko asked of Kyle's fate.

"Nothing. I got this bro. This nigga just tried to tarnish my name and made me look like a fool in front of my brothers. I'm gonna do this nigga myself," Samir instructed.

The rest of the Corleones stood back and wondered if Samir really had the heart to pull the trigger himself. Until now, they were the ones with blood on their hands while Samir gave the orders.

"Tell the devil, I said hello my nigga," Samir told Kyle. Just as the words left his mouth, he raised his Glock forty to Kyle's forehead, looked him dead in his eyes and pulled the trigger, splattering his brains all over the basement wall.

"Oh yeah, and tell him The Black Corleones sent you..."

Chapter Two

The next day, Samir stood in the large bay window of his downtown condo overlooking the majesty of his city. He watched the sun rise across the horizon, and he didn't feel the same. He got into the game to prove himself to his family, and as a way to provide for his crew. He never thought at 17 years old he would be a murderer too. For some reason, he thought he could avoid the violence of the game. But he soon learned that violence and crime goes hand and hand. He admired the mob, and even they killed for the sake of the names they were upholding. He just figured he could make a little money selling dope and avoid any real hick ups. He finally understood what his father meant when he said this was a man's game.

Staring at the sun sparkle off the waves of Lake Michigan, Samir knew he had to accept his new role. It was business, nothing personal. Fact is; if he had to do it again, he would do it in a heartbeat.

He didn't feel like going to school, but he knew his mother would have a heart attack if she got wind of him skipping, so he pulled himself out of his hustler mind frame and headed to first period. He sat in the back of the class, paying no attention to his teacher, yet again. Cesar joined him in class, looking like a walking, talking, dope boy billboard. Samir wasn't into the flashy side of the game. He didn't care for a bunch of jewelry, over the top clothes and overly expensive cars. He was a simple dude, because he believed in drawing less attention to himself as possible.

Even though Samir avoided the limelight, Cesar was all for it. He was a hustler, and he wanted everybody to know it. While Samir steered away from the shine, Cesar ran towards it. He was trying to be low key, but he learned from the talk in the streets that he wasn't as low key as he thought he was, and even though he tried to avoid people knowing his name, everybody knew it, and that was evident from his birthday party.

"Yo, my nigga, do you have to be flashy everywhere you go, I mean, we're at school," Samir whispered.

"I know you ain't talking with those Ferragamo's on your feet," Cesar joked.

"I been wearing this shit since the day I was born, people are familiar to seeing me this way, you, on the other hand bro, are bringing too much attention to yourself."

"Excuse me, Mr. Kendall, is there something you would like to share with the rest of the class, because that conversation must be really important that you have to interrupt my lecture," Samir's teacher interrupted before Cesar could respond.

"No sir. I apologize," he said.

"Good, you may want to pay attention since there is a test coming up that is thirty five percent of your grade, and you do want to graduate this spring. I expect more from my seniors."

Samir hated school and couldn't wait for it to be over. He felt he didn't need the lesson plan because he couldn't use any of it in life, and besides, he had already chosen his career path. After class, he received a message from Tim that he was to be at the Lawrys' restaurant immediately after school. He knew today was his father's weekly co-op meeting, and he had never been invited before. He was nervous as to why the co-op leaders wanted him there. He started thinking the worst as his nerves got the best of him. He had just been dealt a major blow that he was quick to rectify, so he was hoping this invitation didn't have anything to do with the situation with Kyle.

"Bring Meko with you. Don't show up a second late nephew."

Samir forward the message to Meko and headed toward his car. He knew he didn't have to worry about Meko not being there. Meko was becoming his right hand man, and he didn't want to move without him. Even if he didn't get a request for Meko's presence, he would have brought him along anyway. Just as he suspected, Meko was already at his car waiting for him.

"What you think this shit's about bro?" Meko inquired.

"I don't know, but I hope they're not about to tell us they pulling the plug because of this Kyle shit. I'm nervous to be honest."

"Man, don't sweat it bro. With all the money we making your pops and his co-op, they would be fools to pull the plug now; we in too deep."

Samir listened to Meko's point of view and put his thoughts at ease. When his phone rang, he noticed it was Khloe's friend. His excitement grew because he hadn't spoken to her since their date and he was anxious to see her again.

"Hey doll face," he answered.

"Hi Samir, what are you doing?"

"I'm on my way downtown to meet my pops. I've

been thinking of you constantly. Why haven't I heard from you?"

"It's a long story. I had to go home, and I didn't have a way to contact you while I was there," she explained.

"Well, we're gonna have to change all that. When I leave downtown I'm gonna come get you and we'll make sure you can contact me whenever you need me, cool?

"Okay, cool. What time are you going to come, I'm at my friend's house?"

"Give me two hours, baby girl, I'll be there."

"Okay, I miss you, and be careful."

"I miss you too," Samir ended their conversation feeling good. He didn't care that his partner thought he was caking, he just knew he had to see her smile. He couldn't shake the feeling he had for her. He never felt anything toward a female, so he knew this had to mean she was different, and he couldn't wait to see her.

When they arrived at the restaurant, they were escorted to a private dining room where the co-op was already taking place. Once Carlyle noticed his son walk in, he stopped, introduced him to everyone at the table, and instructed them to have a seat.

"I know you are wondering why I called you

here, and as you can see, there are some familiar faces here. As heads of your set you will need to attend all co-op meetings and give a full report on what's going on with your set. If there are issues, they are discussed here," Carlyle explained to Samir and Meko.

If running their sets wasn't hard enough, now they had the added pressure of dealing with the entire co-op. Niggas who had been running Chicago for over 30 years.

"So, young Samir, I heard you had a problem in your neck of the woods, and I'm a little disappointed because those are our most profitable blocks, young gun. Explain to me what the hell is going on over there," Quincy, a longtime member of the co-op and leader of the Joliet and Champagne crews asked.

"Yes, I had a problem with a jack boy, but that's nothing to worry about because my crew and I handled that situation," Samir responded.

"What do you mean when you say handled?" Tim asked.

"What Samir means is, we took care of the situation. We retrieved every dollar and every gram that was lost. Then we sent a little message to anybody else that may be feeling a little froggy," Meko replied.

"So, in less than forty eight hours you found the people responsible and retrieved everything?" Another member asked.

"Yes, we did. There is nothing more important than this family and what the five of us are building. We refuse to allow anyone to bring shame on this family and our Black Corleone legacy," Samir offered his answer.

"Damn Lyle, this young man is solid. You said this was your baby boy. He doesn't carry himself like a baby to me."

"I know, he isn't and I couldn't be more proud of him. He handled a situation when most cats ten years his senior would have folded," Carlyle boasted.

"Samir, we know about the situation and we know that you handled it when you did and that's why you and Meko are sitting at this table right now. So, this is your induction into these meetings. You and Meko are to meet us here every week. Tim will hit you once a week with the time. When you show up, you will need to have a full report on your sets down to what the corner boys are doing. If you can't attend, an acceptable replacement must be here to represent your crew. Do you understand?" He explained.

"Yes sir, we do," Samir responded.

"Good, because you've just entered the big league, son…"

The meeting continued as normal, and Samir and Meko soaked in everything they heard. They observed how the crew conducted themselves and their business. They watched their mannerisms and how they spoke to each other. There was a reason his father and his crew had been in the game as long as they were. They had everything down to a science. It was almost like they were heading fortune 500 companies, and this was a board meeting. They used code words and spoke in corporate terms. If you didn't know who they were, you would never know they were drug lords.

Meko admired the old heads, and in his mind he wanted the Corleones to be exactly like them. He was excited about attending the meetings because he knew he could learn much more from them about running the game. Samir, on the other hand, already knew of his father's way of conducting business, so he wasn't as surprised as Meko, but he was in complete pupil mode. He wanted to make sure he observed as much as he could because he needed to be on point when they attended the meeting the following week.

After the meeting, Meko and Samir headed to the suburbs to meet with Seven. He was busy scouting a new location to move their trap spot. Ever since the robbery, the Corleones didn't feel comfortable operating in the same places out of caution. Seven decided on a location in Riverdale that was just on the outskirts of the small suburb, but still within city limits.

"This is a good location, but make sure we have at least four niggas here at all times, and we need to update the surveillance around here too," Meko said as he looked around the area.

"I'm already on it. I got the tech guys coming out here tomorrow," Seven informed Meko and Samir.

"What's up with Roseland; we get another spot over there yet?" Samir asked.

"Yeah, Ces found a spot on one eleventh and Parnell. He over there now getting the spot wired with cameras and shit," Seven replied.

"Aight cool, you and Chase go over there and check everything out, and hit me. I'm gonna fuck with y'all a little later, I got something important to handle. Meko, hang out with Seven and let him in on the meeting we went to today."

"Cool, I got you. I was gon' fuck with this nigga anyway."

Samir left his compadres to take care of the business while he headed to see his ray of sunshine. Shit was becoming hectic in his world and he needed something to relax his mind so he wouldn't go crazy. His peace would remain intact, and he couldn't think of anything or anyone better to do that with than Khloe.

His palms began to sweat and his heart pounded in his chest when he arrived to her friend's house. He sat there for a good five minutes trying to calm his nerves before he called her outside. *Damn, what the hell is wrong with me, calm down Samir, you are Sam Corleone, and this girl got you tripping.* He thought to himself. He snapped out of his nervousness and called her.

"Hello?" her friend Shay answered.

"Yo, what's up, can I speak with Miss Khloe please?" he asked.

"Is this Samir?"

"Yea, it is. Is she still there?"

"Oh My God, heeeeey Samir, yes, she's here. Hold on one second," Shay laughed, "It's your maaaan, bitch," she handed Khloe the phone.

"Girl, stop being silly, he's not my man, we just met. Hey, Samir," Khloe said simultaneously to the both of them.

"So, I'm not your man now? Damn, I need to step my game up," Samir teased.

"I mean, we just met, I didn't think about it. Where are you?"

"Well, I am your man from here on out if that's what it takes to stop somebody from stealing your heart from me. And I'm outside, you ready?

"Yes, I'm ready. Give me one second, I'm coming out," She said as she smiled harder than she ever smiled. She quickly hung up the phone and grabbed her stuff.

"Girl, what are you so happy about?" Shay asked.

"Samir is outside, and he just told me he was my man," she laughed.

"Whoop, Whoop! Well, don't keep *your man* waiting," Shay joked.

Khloe tried to keep her composure when she walked outside and saw him standing against his car, looking good. He was dressed in Coogi Australia from top to bottom. She ran and jumped in his arms as if she was a little girl jumping into the arms of Santa Claus. She kissed him passionately because the truth was, she really missed him, and couldn't stop thinking of him since the day she first met him.

"Damn, what was that for?" he smiled.

"I just miss you, and I'm happy to see you, that's all."

"Well, I miss you too, Miss Khlo," He said as he helped her into his car.

For the first time in a long time Samir was at

peace; Khloe brought out a side of him that he didn't know he possessed. All the cares of the world melted away when he was near her. He felt himself staring at her as he drove. Without thinking, he grabbed her hand and kissed it gently as they sat at a red light on 115th and Halstead. She looked at him and smiled. She knew at that very moment that her otherwise miserable young life would change now that Samir was a part of it.

"I'm glad you came, Samir," she broke their silence.

"I told you I would be here. You never have to worry about me not coming. I wouldn't miss an opportunity to be next to you for nothing in the world."

"Where are we going anyways?"

"Where ever you want to go. But first, I thought we go to River Oaks mall and get you a two-way, so you don't have an excuse not to call me."

"Can we get clothes too?" she asked, giving him her best puppy dog face.

He laughed out loud at her attempt to play on his emotions, "We can buy the entire mall if you want to, as long as I don't have to see that pitiful face you got on right now."

They headed toward Samir's favorite suburban mall. He stopped at the Sprint Store to get her a

Nextel phone and a Motorola two-way, and then he followed her into every store she liked. He watched in awe as she looked through the racks of Man Alive and picked out her clothes. Every once in a while she would ask him if she could have different things, and each time he told her she could have whatever she wanted if it made her happy.

During their first shopping spree Samir spent close to $8000 on everything; from Pelle Pelle, Coogi, Guess, Airforce Ones and Jordans. He made sure she got everything her heart desired without thinking twice. As they were about to leave, Samir made one more stop. He walked into Zales and dropped another $3500 on a diamond heart necklace that was just as beautiful as he thought Khloe was. It sparkled the way her smiled sparkled to him.

"Did you get your pretzel Miss Lady?" he asked as she approached him, coming out of the jewelry store.

"Yes, I did, sir. But I'm hungry, can we go to Bennigans, I saw one across the street?"

"Of Course we can. I got something else for you too," he told her as they were seated inside the restaurant. He pulled out the jewelry boxed and her eyes lit up. He opened the box and revealed the necklace he just purchased for her.

"Oh my God, Samir it's beautiful. You bought this for me?"

"Yea, because I think you're beautiful, it's my heart, so I hope you like it."

"I do, I love it," she said, but her excitement immediately turned into sadness as she thought about the current state of her life.

"What's wrong babe?" he asked her.

"Nothing, it's just... I never had anybody in my life be this nice to me."

"Tell me that long story you mentioned earlier," he said, grabbing her hand.

"It's just that my home life is horrible. My mother is physically and emotionally abusive. She makes me hate my life. So, when you say I'm beautiful, I don't see it because no one ever tells me that. I run away, but she always finds me and makes me come back, and then she kicks me out again. Sometimes I wish I could just die so I don't have to feel so bad anymore," she told him as the tears filled her eyes.

Samir got up and joined her on her side of the booth. He put his arm around her and sat in silence for a moment. He would have never guessed that this beautiful young girl felt so ugly on the inside. He made a silent vow to himself that if it took his whole life he would show her how beautiful she really was. He wanted to be her superman at that very moment.

"Listen, Khlo, don't worry about that shit no more. I'm here for you, and I always will be, I promise. If you need me, I'll be there, no matter what I'm doing; I'll be there. Okay, don't cry baby, you got me."

They spent the rest of the day together. No phones, no two-way pagers, no drug game, nothing; just him and her. He wanted to make her happy even if it was just for one day.

When they arrived back at Shay's house, he didn't want to let her go. He wanted her to stay with him forever. Since she told him all about what was going on in her world, he wanted to protect her from any pain she felt.

"You gon' be okay over here, right?" he asked her.

"Yes babe, I'll be fine," she kissed him goodnight and went inside.

He didn't know it then, but this would be the last time he saw her for a long while. He watched as she retreated into the house safely, and right then his serenity was over. He had to go back to being Sam Corleone.

Chapter Three

In a somber mood and with Khloe on his mind, Samir met with Seven for the second time that day. They stood outside of the Robert Taylor projects hanging out when Seven noticed something was amiss about Samir's demeanor. He couldn't help but wonder if the trial of the dope life was getting to his brother and leader.

"Yo, what's on your mind, my nigga?" Seven asked as he passed a swisher Samir's way.

"I just got a lot on my mind with pops inviting us to the co-op meetings, and with all eyes being on us. I been trying to keep my name out these streets, but the truth is; everybody knows who I am, and on top of all that, I gotta go see my brother's tomorrow."

"I know, this shit is tough and it's getting to me too, Joe, but we in this shit together. We got your back no matter the situation. Just relax, we doing what we set out to do," Seven tried to assure him.

"You remember that shorty I met the other day, Joe?"

"Yea, I remember, what about her?"

"I'm really feeling her, but she going through some bogus shit at home, plus she young as shit."

"Oh yeah, like what kinda shit?"

"Man, Joe, her mom beats her and shit. She told me today that she feels like she wants to die sometimes. She's beautiful as hell to me, and she's going through some fucked up shit. I can only see her when she runs away to her best friend's house."

"Damn, how old is she?"

"Young bro, she is hella young."

"How young, my nigga?" Seven insisted.

"I can't even tell you how young she is. Plus, I'm about to be eighteen in a couple of weeks.

"Bro, if you feeling her that strongly to be worried about her, then fuck how old she is. Age ain't shit but a number, bro."

"You right, but when I turn eighteen she would be barely a teenager, bro. She would barely be a freshman when we're about graduate."

"Damn, that is young. But fuck it, the heart wants what the heart wants. She young as hell, but you can mold her."

"Yea, you right, if I get to see her again. I bought

her a phone and shit, so she can hit me when she needs me. It's tough knowing that she going through that shit and I can't do nothing about it," he said as he took another pull of his blunt.

"Don't trip bro, she'll hit you. I'm sure of it."

"I hope so, because when I'm around her my mind is at ease. All the bullshit of this crazy life just goes away. Feel me?"

"I do bro, I feel that way about Kaiyah. Shorty eases my hectic ass mind. I knew she was my bitch after that shit with Kyle, and without saying a word, she just looked at me, kissed me and held me. That shit was the best feeling in the world. To be around somebody who helps you forget about our crazy ass street life even if it's just for the moment."

"Yeah, I know what you mean. I feel like that when I'm with her. I just hope I can see her again," Samir said as he thought of his situation with Khloe. He felt helpless because he wanted nothing more than to make sure she was happy at all times, but all he could do was sit and wait.

Samir hung out a little longer with Seven and some niggas he knew from around the way before he headed home. It had been a crazy few days, and he hadn't seen much of his mother in a while. But when he arrived to her house, she was already asleep. So he did what he did every night he went over to check on her. He kissed her on her forehead, and as he turned to leave, she woke up.

"Samir, love, are you okay?" she asked him in a very low tone.

"Yea, lady, I'm okay. I was just coming to check on you, but you were sleep."

"Come here Samir, let's talk awhile."

He obeyed his mother and sat on the edge of the bed next to her. She looked at him and she could sense something was bothering him. He could hide it from everyone on the streets, but she knew him better than he knew himself.

"So, tell me, what's wrong love?"

"I just got a lot going on mom. This game ain't easy, and I'm finding myself having to be another person to handle this. Plus, there's this girl."

"This girl?" she interrupted him.

"Yea, I met this girl a few days ago, and I really like her, but her home life is crazy and I feel helpless. I want to protect her, but I can't. I just gotta wait until she calls me. I don't like that feeling because something in me needs her around all the time and I don't know why," he explained to his mother. She smiled hard while she listened to him pour his heart out over a girl. She never seen him with a girl that he actually liked. He had never brought anyone home, so this girl had to be special;

even for him to mention her.

"Well, first thing first, you have to be cautious out here in these streets, son. You can't let yourself be so caught up in the game that it starts to affect your peace. I was worried that this would begin to weigh on you, and you're so young, but it's a choice you made. But you can always choose to not let it stress you. I hear what people have to say, and you are doing things out there most people take a lifetime to do. So, be the boss son, and bosses put other people in place to handle things they don't want to."

"As far as this girl is concerned, it sounds like my baby boy is smitten. If you like her, just be there for her when she does call. Things will work out. You will get your chance to be her knight in shining armor, you just wait and see," she expressed while hugging him.

Samir loved how his mother was able to make everything sound so much better. He needed this talk with her. She always had a way of lifting the weight of the world off his shoulders with her words. He kissed her good night and headed home. He thought about Khloe most of the night. No matter what he did, he couldn't get her out of his mind. He saw her face when he closed his eyes, and felt her presence in his heart.

"This must be what love at first sight feels like cuz I can't stop thinking about you. Just thought you should know. Goodnight". He messaged her.

Goodnight Samir, I miss you baby and I'm thinking of you too. Thank you for an amazing day. She responded instantly.

He smiled when he read her message and knowing he was on her mind as much as she was on his helped him sleep better that night.

The next morning, he woke up bright and early because it was visitation day. He didn't expect to be visiting his brothers today, but of course he had too, due to the situation he found himself in with Kyle. He knew Sincere was not happy, and frankly he didn't want to deal with Sin telling him what he should of did and what he needed to do. He had a good handle on his operation, but with his brothers being locked up, they couldn't witness the leaps and bounds Samir was making within his reign.

He got dressed in his normal visitation prep gear. He decided to wear a cardigan from Valentino, a purple label polo shirt, jeans and a pair of Roberto Cavalli sneakers. He opted to leave his jewelry out of his ensemble for the visit.

Once he was dressed, he stood in his massive picture window and gathered his thoughts. His favorite *Jay Z* album played loudly through his Bose speakers. He used the melodies to help him clear his mind. The truth was; the game was taking a toll on him early. His father and brothers warned him that this life wouldn't be easy, but Samir's legacy was growing faster than he imagined, and with more money, came more responsibility, and more problems.

Music Playing

"And ain't nothing changed so even in my afterlife I sew it up/ Don't grieve for me my art remains/ Like a dart from the speaker to your heart/ Spiritually through the portal now my words is immortal/ Don't plan to leave without a fight/ I plant a seed I give life/ Though I can't see past the girls greed to call her wife/ Next time you're thinking heist better be precise/ Cause I'm fully prepared. One of us is gon' leave here/ I have no regrets/even tho I won't see grow my godson Boogie, Sonny and Remo/ Lucky Me."

As the chorus played, he was beginning to think nobody understood what it was like to be Samir Corleone. Or even what it took to be Samir Kendall. He had the eyes of streets on him at all times, and if

35

that wasn't enough pressure, he had to live up to his father's and his older brother's reputation. He was the baby, and that's how the dope world viewed him. He was desperate to come out of their shadows and run his business without them being on top of him, micro managing his every move. He was hoping that after the way he handled himself in the first test of his true leadership in the game, his father and brothers would trust that he could handle himself and let go of the reigns they held onto so tightly.

He stared out at his view of Lake Michigan and let the music massage his mental. Nobody fully understood how he felt at this moment.

You only know what you see/ You don't understand what it takes to be me/ You only know what you see/ You don't understand what it takes to me.

As the song began to fade out, Samir grabbed his key's and headed out the door. He turned and looked at his plush Neo-Italian furnished apartment and thought about where he started, and where he was headed, and he found the strength to keep pushing toward the legacy he had just begun to start.

"Lucky me." he said to himself as he headed out the door.

Chapter Four

Samir pulled into the parking lot of the Cook County Jail. He was just as nervous as he was over a year ago when he first told his brothers he was joining the game. He spent his whole life trying to impress Sincere. He never wanted to look like a fool in front of his eldest brother. Even though he wished it didn't; Sincere's opinion of him held major weight his entire life, and he knew he was in for a disappointed conversation from Sin.

He took a deep breath and headed inside the jail, just to get it over with. His palms began to sweat as he waited in the visitation room for his brothers to come out. When he noticed them enter the room, his heart dropped to the pit of his stomach. Sin and Ace didn't seem like they were too upset with him, but he knew his brothers well enough to know that they always kept their cool.

"What's up fam, how y'all feeling?" Samir broke

the ice.

"We good Sam, what's good with you?" Ace asked.

"Let's stop all the small talk. What the fuck happened out there?" Sin jumped in.

"To make a long story short, we got approached to front, Meko was apprehensive, but we voted, and the nigga stuck us up."

"How did you let that happen, Corleone?" Ace asked his little brother.

"First of all, I didn't let anything happen. It just happened. The nigga had a vendetta, and he stuck us up."

"Samir, I don't think you ready for this game. That's too big of a loss," Sin doubted his little brother.

"No disrespect, but don't tell me what the fuck I'm ready for. Niggas was so quick to report word that I got hit, but did niggas come down here and report that I found the niggas responsible in less than twenty four hours, and recovered all that was taking, down to the last gram?"

Sin and Ace sat in silence, dumbfounded that their baby brother had such a handle on things.

"Naw, that report ain't make it to us until just now. Don't think we being hard on you, we just want you to protect your name and your rep out here, Sam. This shit is tough for me sitting in this fucking cell when I should be out here grooming you and protecting you. So, when I heard that shit happened, I was angrier than I would have been if I was on the streets. You're my baby brother, and I'm not out here guiding you, and that shit fucks with me every day," Sincere explained.

"Samir, you gotta understand that we believe in you whole heartedly, and we know you can do this, shit... look where you got in a year. But it's like this, we taught you how to tie your shoes, ride a bike, how to drive, and now you in the game and we in this fucking box. If anything happened to you, I'd be lost, little bro," Ace chimed in.

"I get where y'all are coming from, but y'all gon' have to let me grow up. I'm gonna be graduating in a few months and turning eighteen soon after that, so I think it's time y'all let me do me, and trust that I can handle myself," he implored.

"That's just it, I gotta let my baby bro grow up in the game without me," Sin said.

They talked for the rest of the visit, but once it was over, Sin and Ace retreated back to their cell, not wanting to let go of the hold they had on Samir. But they understood that it was time they let him grow up. That didn't mean they wouldn't make sure he was well taken care of in the streets.

They had to trust that he knew what he was doing, and that he could deal with whatever the game had to offer. Their baby brother was his own man in the dope game, and they just had to come to terms with it, one way or another.

Samir couldn't let his family's constant need to protect him keep him from building his brand in his chosen profession. He put things off long enough. In order to prove that he could handle his task, Samir had to make a move that would solidify who he was in his rise to the top, once and for all.

It was time to venture into parts unknown. It was time for The Corleones to head to Houston and get acquainted with the southern dope market.

He put the idea to rest for a later time, but with the streets buzzing about what he would do next, he knew this was the only way he could prove that being a Kendall had nothing to do with his success, but everything to do with being a Black Corleone.

A few months passed and things were starting to get back to normal for the Black Corleones. Their location moves had proven to be more beneficial to them than they thought. They were moving so much work that Carlyle decided to expand their territories into his low-end sets, and into the north side of the city. He even trusted the Corleones to venture into his Calumet City and Indiana territories.

Samir and the Corleones practically ran all of the south suburban sets, as well as most of the south side city sets while his brother Keith ran all of the west side, east side and most of the north side Chicago sets. Carlyle Kendall's youngest son had stepped up to the plate harder than he could imagine, and he couldn't be more proud.

Samir was finally getting into a flow with his operation, and the hang-ups he experienced had become a blur. Although things had calmed down significantly, the streets knew that double crossing the Corleones would be detrimental after the discovery of Kyle and his Crew's dismantled bodies. He had sent the very messaged he needed to send in order for his operation to get back on track and running smoothly. Dealing was becoming the forefront of his life, and graduation couldn't come any sooner. Samir and his crew were 2 months away from their high school graduation when he approached them about his plans to go down south.

"So, I've been thinking for a while now about going down to Houston, and moving our shit out there," Samir informed his crew during their weekly meetings.

"What the hell for?" Cesar replied as he rolled his blunt.

"I know a few niggas out there who need a solid connect with some good work, cuz' they shit is stepped on hard. So, I figure we go out there and see what's up. The going rate down south is fifteen five, so if we go down there with the shit we got at twelve five, we'll make a fucking killing."

"And how long you been contemplating this shit, cuz I know you ain't just come up with it out the blue?" Seven inquired.

"Naw, I been thinking about it for a long while, since before that shit with Kyle, but the timing wasn't right, then we had that little hang up. But it's time we at least make a trip. Plus, shorty I was fucking with linked me with a few niggas who fucked with my brothers and they're ready."

"When?" Cesar asked.

"I was thinking we go down there for spring break and set shit up; have it pumping by middle summer."

"But what about your pops, don't we have to clear it with him and the co-op first?" Chase asked.

"Y'all let me handle my pops. Me and Meko will meet with him and then bring it up at the next co-op meeting. But with the money we been making them niggas, they can't refuse."

"Let's just do what we do and put it to a vote. All in favor with Samir's plan to go see what's up with Houston vote yay. All those not in favor, vote nay," Meko called his crew to their votes.

"Yay," Seven voted first

"Cool with me." Cesar voted next.

"Yea, why not," Chase continued the vote.

Meko went last with the final vote that put them all in agreement with their reigning leader. Samir was excited that his crew was down with his idea to take their operation to a higher level. He knew this was what they needed to prove themselves once and for all.

The only thing left to do was to inform his father of his plans, and to get the okay from the co-op. This Houston trip was exactly what Samir needed to really stand apart from the rest of the Kendall's and he was determined to make sure it would be an opportunity of a lifetime. Little did he know, venturing down south would make his name bigger than his older brothers, and it would be his defining moment. Expanding into uncharted territory would be the decision that would set the Corleones on a course neither of them could ever imagine.

Samir wrapped up his meeting, and as all of his fellas began to file out, Carla arrived to see him.

Samir had plenty of women, but he never felt what he was beginning to feel for Khloe. Normally he would be content with Carla's presence because her pussy was amazing, and the things she did with her mouth were mind blowing, but this time he didn't feel any type of way about her at all. He was just going to fuck her and send her on her way.

"Yo, Sam, I'ma fuck with you tomorrow," Meko smirked as he looked at Carla.

"Aight Joe, lets link up tomorrow for breakfast," Samir responded.

"Hey Meko," Carla said sarcastically.

"What up doe, Carla," Meko laughed in her face as he made his exit.

"Hey Samir, baby," Carla greeted Samir and tried to kiss his cheek, but he moved away. "What's wrong with you?" She asked.

"Nothing, you know we ain't on no kissing each other and baby type of level," he told her.

"Wait, Samir, I been fucking you for quite some time now."

"Key word, fucking. Not my wifey, just fucking me."

"What, did you have a bad day in the hood, cuz' you're being awfully mean."

"I am not being mean, I told you before, I don't want to get our signals crossed. I like fucking you, but I'm not fucking with you, and you said you were cool with that. So, now your tune changed or some shit?"

"No, I am cool with it. Let's not talk about it anymore. Let's get naked and have wild crazy sex, and fall asleep like we always do," she said as she started to unzip his pants in the middle of his kitchen. His dick began to rise as she massaged it, trying to take her mind off the unpleasantness of their conversation. But just as she was about to take all of him in her mouth, his two-way went off. *I miss you Samir and I need you.* Khloe messaged him.

Carla was trying her best to give him the kind of head that usually made his toes curl, but this time his mind was much too preoccupied, and when he realized Khloe was messaging him, he immediately pushed Carla away, zipped his pants, and headed to his living room.

"Hello," she answered.

"Khlo, baby, what's the matter?" he immediately responded.

"Nothing, I'm at my friend's house. I'm sorry I haven't called. I had to go home, and I left my phone and stuff here so my mother wouldn't take it."

"It's cool, baby. I miss you too though."

45

"Where are you? Is it too late for you to come and see me?" she asked."

"It's never too late for you, Khlo. I'm on my way," he told her as he hung up the phone.

Carla was furious. *How could he just play her like this when he knew she wanted to be with him?* To just up and run to another chick while she was standing right in front of him killed her. But she knew she had to play it cool, because if it wasn't for Samir, she would not be able to afford her lifestyle, and she would be out on the streets.

Carla was on the verge of losing everything her mother left her when Samir approached her about using her home as a stash spot. So, she couldn't risk losing her income, and she most certainly couldn't do anything to double cross him. She just had to deal with the fact that his interest was elsewhere.

"So, you just gon' bounce like that? Samir, you bogus as hell," she pouted.

"Carla, I don't have time for this shit. Just get your stuff and let's roll."

"Who is she, Samir?" she asked.

"Excuse me? You gotta be kidding me, right? Don't fucking question me, Carla, but if you must know, she's something you're not," Samir told her, becoming agitated with her presence. "I tell you what, this little sex shit we doing; we can dead all that. I'm done with it. I'm good. So, please, be a lady and leave," he told her, opening the door for her to remove herself.

Carla didn't say a word; she just grabbed her purse and headed out the door. But as she was leaving, he grabbed her by the arm and told her not to let her emotions get her killed. She wouldn't do anything to fuck him over, but he had to make sure, especially with everything that happened with Kyle.

Once she was gone, he grabbed his keys and headed to the wild hundreds.

Music Playing

Loving you is all I need/ Never take your love from me/ Cuz I think I would lose my mind if you would go away/ So say your never leave my side/ That forever you'll be mines/ April Shower me with your love.

Dru hill danced across his Chevy speakers like poetry. Every time he listened to that particular song he thought of her. It was the one song that expressed exactly how he was beginning to feel. Even though he didn't get to see her often, and had only seen her once since their shopping trip, he was falling in love with her. He was never supposed to let love get in the way. Frankly, he didn't have time for it. But all of that went out the window the day Khloe walked in Harold's.

When he pulled up to Shay's house, he felt that school crush nervousness. He called her outside, but this time instead of her jumping in his arms, he walked over to her and picked her up off her feet, holding onto her for dear life. She threw her arms around him and nuzzled her face in his neck, inhaling his cologne. At that very moment they were at peace.

"Damn, I really missed you, Khlo," he expressed to her once they were inside the car.

"I missed you too. I wish we can be together all the time, but I know my momma gonna make me come home soon, and I won't get to see you," she pouted.

"Just take your pager with you and hide it from her. Whenever you need me, I'll come out to the hills for you."

"Really, you would come way to country club hills to see me?" she asked, excited.

"I'd go to the moon if you were there," he said as he kissed her cheek. And just as she felt his soft lips touch her face, she turned and kissed him passionately. His dick grew in excitement, but he gained his composure and ended their make out session. He didn't know her status, and he wanted to take things slow with her in case she was still a virgin. With her being so young, he didn't want to rush it. He was just happy being near her.

"So, you ate yet?" he asked her.

"No, I haven't, and I am hungry. Ooh, can we go to Portillo's, I love their cheese fries?" she asked, with a huge smile on her face.

"Yeah, we can go there, love," he laughed at her happiness.

They headed downtown for Italian beefs and cheese fries. As they sat in his car talking and enjoying each other's company, he finally opened up to her and told her how much he adored her and wanted her to be in his life. She was beautiful in his eyes, and she made his otherwise ugly world beautiful too.

Khloe had never had anyone make her feel as special as Samir did. For the first time in her young life she mattered to someone, and that was the best feeling in the world to her. She secretly made a vow to always be by his side, no matter what. She couldn't imagine being anywhere else in the world but with him.

He drove her back to her friend's house before it got too late, but before she went inside, he played her song.

"Hey, Khlo, I want you to hear this song. It's the song I listen to when I miss you," he played *April Showers* for her, and as the melody played, she began to cry because he was so amazing to her. He didn't have to be there for her, and just to know someone out there cared for her was overwhelming.

Music Playing

And girl I'll give you all the love I have/ Inside this heart of mine/ And yes I swear that I'll be here for you/ Forever and all times/ So if ever you feel lonely/All you have to do is call me/ And I'll be there to shower you with my love.

She listened to every word and held the song deep in her heart. She leaned over and kissed him slowly before she retreated back inside. As she was getting out the car, he grabbed her hand.

"If ever you feel lonely, all you have to do is call me," he smiled, reciting the lyrics of her song. She smiled, kissed him one more time and headed inside. With that kiss it was official that Samir Corleone was in love.

Chapter Five

Things began to look up in Samir's world. He found the girl of his dreams, and his business was running better than he could have imagined.

With the new trap locations, Samir and his crew tripled their profit margin. Spring break was rolling around quickly and the weather in Chicago was beginning to break. Samir and Meko continued their weekly co-op meetings, and doing so they gained the respect of all the elders. With a break from school approaching, Samir figured it would be a perfect time for them to put the wheels in motion for his down south plans. Since their last conversation about expansion, he decided that New Orleans would be a perfect place for them to venture to as well. He had a couple of associates trying to convince him to come to the Crescent City, so he decided that it was worth checking out. They would spend 3 days in Houston and 3 days in New

Orleans.

He wasn't worried about his father not allowing him to go forward with the southern expansion. He was more worried about the work load, and if he could handle it. He didn't have many issues supplying out of town clientele, but then again, he wasn't moving the way those niggas moved. This situation would be different, because it wouldn't be the same as him running his sets in Chicago. This venture was going to require multiple trips back and forth, and it was going to put more pressure on The Corleones who were already dealing with taking over Chicago. Samir was optimistic about it and knew they could handle it.

He walked into his father's house nervous about dropping another bomb on him, but just like his induction into the game, he was expanding, with or without his father's approval. This was the move Samir needed to set him apart from his family ties, so he wasn't going to allow anybody to stand in his way.

"What's up pops?"

"Sam, what's going on with you?" his father asked.

Samir didn't say anything as he watched two plain clothed mean leave out of his father's basement.

"Who is that dad?" he inquired.

"Oh, that's just a few alphabet boys your pops has on the payroll. They were just informing me of an upcoming raid in one of our neighborhoods."

"It's not one of my neighborhoods is it?" Samir asked.

"Don't worry about it, son. When it's your turn, you'll be well prepared for it."

"Okay, cool. Pops, I been thinking about making a trip down south this spring break. I have a few things I want to set in motion in Houston and in N.O., but I had to make sure you were cool with it first," Samir explained.

"Okay, what's the plan for this trip, Samir Kendall?"

"I got a few people down there that I want to put in position to allow me to expand into the down south market. The prices down there are nice, and if I come in at lower prices I know we can make a killing. We just gon' go down there, set everything up, and start moving," Samir explained to his father.

"I don't know about this, Samir. I know your crew been doing big things around the city, but I feel better with you being here. Expanding means you have to spend time down there to make sure shit is running smoothly, and I don't know if I could protect you in areas outside of my reach. How about I let you expand out in New York and Virginia. I can protect you there."

"With all respect, Dad, I'm not feeling going into your market. I appreciate the fact that you got my back, but if I'm gon' be in this game, I need to make my own name. I need to know what I can do on my own. Honestly, I know a lot of my success is because of my last name. Down there it's just me and the Corleones. I need this to solidify myself pops, and expand our business as a crew. Don't worry, you gonna make money with this venture. Just trust me, and understand that I can handle this."

"So, this is really something you think you wanna do?"

"It's something I have to do as a man, pops. You remember how you came up. Imagine if you and your co-op had somebody always putting a cap on what ya'll wanted to do. Do you think you would be where you are today?"

"Say no more, son. Go do what you got to do, but the return deadline remains the same. You're expected to have all the money when it's due, no questions asked. I don't care how shit is going here in the city or down there, the money is due when it's due."

"I understand, dad." Samir agreed.

"Cool, so, is this the only reason you came to visit your old man? I mean, you can hang out with your dad, it ain't always gotta be business," Carlyle told him.

"Naw pops, that's not the only reason I came through. I did wanna talk to you man to man about this girl I met."

"I see. What's on your mind?"

"See, I met her a little while ago, and I'm really feeling her, but she's young, and her home life is crazy. Her mother is abusive towards her, and the only time I really get to see her is when she runs away to her best friend's house, or when her mom kicks her out. I don't know what to do, cuz' I wanna take care of her, but I can't. Like, how do you know you found the one pops? How do you distinguish between real love and strong like?" Samir asked his father.

"Sounds like a tough one, Samir. I remember when I first met your mother. The very moment I saw her on campus something inside of me ignited and I had to have that woman. See, meeting her made me feel something I never felt. I was usually only concerned about what a woman would be like in bed, but when I met your momma, I found myself just wanting to be next to her. I would drive down to Champagne to see her every chance I got. I spent hours thinking about her and talking to her. Shit, I never talked to no bitch on the phone when I was that age. It was all about getting money, but your momma, boy, she made me want to hustler harder, just to give her the world," Carlyle explained as he reminisced on his early years with Lola.

"That's exactly how I feel about Khloe, pops. I think I love her."

"Love is a strong emotion, son."

"I know it is, and I know we're both young, but I really think I'm in love with her, and that's kinda scary in this business, because love can get you fucked up."

"Samir, let me tell you something about this game that your older brother's neglected to tell you because they weren't in that mind frame. Being in the game is stressful, and being top guys makes it that much more stressful. You gotta watch everything and everybody. It's a lot about this game that will drive a nigga crazy, so you need to find someone who you know gon' be down for you, and can be your peace away from this game. You need someone there that allows you to leave the stress of the game at the door. If I didn't have that in your momma and your step mother, I wouldn't have lasted this long. Losing your mother was the hardest thing I had to deal with, and if I could change it, I would, but I was lucky cuz' I found your step mother, and I'm even luckier that we have the kind of family dynamic that we have, and that son, is credit to the kind of woman your mother is."

"I feel that, but how do I have that with her if I can't even see her?"

"You just got to be patient with that situation, son, especially if you say you in love with her. Just take what you can and the time will come. All you gotta do is be patient."

"I'm trying, pops, but sometimes I just want to be with her and I can't."

"Trust me, I know the feeling, but just listen to your old man, I won't steer you wrong."

"Aight pops. Thanks for the advice. Let me get outta here, I gotta meet up with the fellas and discuss this trip, so I'll be seeing you, dad."

"How much do you think you're gonna need for that issue?"

"I don't know yet, we just going down there to assess the situation, but I'll have a good idea of what I need when we get back."

"Okay, and when are you planning to go down there?"

"We're going for spring break. We're not

planning to move too much right now. But this summer we'll have it flowing like a river. Once we graduate, we'll have the time to be more hands on with the expansion."

"Make sure you keep me informed, son."

Samir left his father's house ready for spring break to arrive so they could hit the ground running with their down south expansion. He called his down south crew and let them know that he was coming within the next week. The Black Corleones were about become continental, literally.

Running a different city in a different state was going to present challenges for the young crew, but it was a challenge they were all the more ready for, because the money was going to be more than right.

Spring Break week approached quickly and the Corleones met at Samir's condo before sunrise for the 18 hour drive to Houston. Samir barely slept the night before because he was anxious about their impending trip. He knew they had the ability to succeed, because they had proven it to themselves over and over again, but he was still a bit nervous. Everybody in Chicago knew he had the heart of a hustler, but Houston and Louisiana was outside of his cushy life in the Chi. Being a Kendall gave him added security to reign as he pleased, but venturing into territory outside of the Kendall's scope would prove if Samir and the Corleones were built for this, or really just succeeding because of Samir's blood line.

"What up, Joe, you ready for this trip?" Meko asked as they entered Samir's apartment.

"I'm as ready as I'm gon' to be," he responded.

"Aight then, cuz' once we hit this road, ain't no turning back. Is everything ready to go down there?" Meko asked.

"Yea, I spoke with my people last night, so they ready for us to get down there and set everything in motion."

"Is this about us as a crew or about you trying to come out of your pops shadow; cuz' honestly, I don't see why we gotta go down south when we good right here," Cesar said.

The rest of the Corleones looked at Cesar in shock. They couldn't believe his line of questioning.

"What the fuck is that supposed to mean, Ces? Nothing we do is about one man over the next. We voted, and as I recall, you were good with this expansion," Seven replied.

"I know what I did, but I feel like we making a lot of quick decisions, and I'm making sure we ain't feeding into one man's ego."

"*My ego?* You've known me my whole life, and

you know I've never been an egotistical nigga, and for you to ask me some shit like this, it don't sit well with me, so if you got something to say, then you need to say it now, Joe," Samir said calmly.

"I'm just making sure this is for the betterment of the family and not about Sam Corleone. Niggas been moving like we ain't the ones out here grinding. The Black Corleones are The Black Corleones, and not Samir and The Black Corleones. Niggas ain't winning cuz' of one nigga; niggas are winning cuz' we're a crew."

"Cesar, you a hoe ass nigga for this shit; we've always been about each other. When you put us in a fucked up situation, this nigga Sam took the responsibility for your dog ass, and stood up to the co-op, his father and his brothers behind your ass. So, to have you sitting here questioning a nigga like he ain't always had our back... nigga, I swear if you wasn't my brother, I would fuck your bitch ass up, right now. If it wasn't for this nigga, none of us would be where we at. You fucking hoes you couldn't fuck before, driving whips you couldn't afford, and wearing jewelry no nigga in your fam could get," Meko snapped as he became more and more furious with Cesar.

"Really, I'm a hoe ass nigga, Mek? I been a hunit ass nigga since day one, and frankly, this shit been more and more about Sam than the rest of us, and if we going down south then it need to be about us, and not this nigga."

"Don't sit here and talk family to me and then turn around and insinuate the shit you insinuating. Sounds like you the one who ain't about family. You been about the spotlight since the day we started. If it was up to me, your bitch ass wouldn't be a part of this family, because frankly my nigga, the only thing snakes can breed is another snake," Meko said as he approached Cesar before Chase stepped in.

"Chill out Mek, Cesar, you out of line for this shit though. Everything we do is about this family, and if any man feel we ain't about our family, or has his own agenda, then he need to leave," Chase interjected.

"Before we hit this road, let me clear this shit up now. Cesar, you been down with me since I was in diapers, my nigga, so don't you ever question my motives again. I could have linked up with my brother's people but I didn't, I came to you niggas. When my own father and brothers were against me bringing you in; I stood up for you, my nigga. This has always been about us, it never been about me, because I was gon' eat with or without you at the end of the day, I'm Samir Kendall before I'm Samir

Corleone. There's no one man above this crew, and when you get out of your fucking prideful ass ways, maybe you'll see that my loyalty lies with this family. But the next time you question my integrity, bro, I promise you, Meko, Seven or Chase won't be able to pull me off your ass. And being that you've known me the longest, you know I mean what I say, and I say what I mean," Samir responded.

Samir turned and walked away in disgust because he knew if he stayed any longer he would do something he regretted. Now was not the time for Cesar to add any negativity to the mix. Samir knew this was Cesar's personality, and lately his behavior was getting to him, but he didn't have time to process Cesar's issue. They had to focus on the expansion; he would deal with Cesar later.

Meko, on the other hand, wasn't easily deterred. He could sense Cesar was becoming exactly like the people he came from, but he knew Samir wouldn't believe that the money they were making was beginning to change Cesar. He didn't want to say anything at the moment because he knew his brother was upset, even if he didn't show it.

At that very moment Meko made a decision to watch Cesar a little closer. He put a call into his solider Carlos to gather some info on Cesar's dealings by the time the Corleones made it back from their trip.

"I don't want you to think for a second that I'm not down with you, Joe. You know how I am, so I wanted to make sure this was us expanding together. The streets are talking, and all they saying is your name," Cesar explained to Samir upon entering his office.

"I don't give a fuck what the streets got to say. Niggas gon' say what they want, but you should know what it is amongst this family. This thing is structured the way it is for a reason, and you too busy worrying about what niggas got to say. I'm disappointed in you, for real, you bogus as hell. Maybe you should stop hanging with niggas that ain't on our level. Niggas too busy trying to be chiefs when they really just Indians," Samir responded.

"I apologize, bro. Let's just hit this road," Cesar reluctantly offered a less than sincere apology.

Fact was; he was beginning to feel vexed about not being considered the top guy, and he felt he could run their operation much more effectively than Samir, but he would have to settle for being number two which was quickly being stripped from him by Meko. Samir was calling on Meko a lot more lately, and Cesar wasn't too happy about it. Samir, on the other hand didn't think anything of what was going on because he accepted Cesar for who he was as a person. He's always been the way he is, ever since they were kids. He never let himself be average. If somebody had something, then Cesar felt he had to have something bigger and better. Once again, Samir brushed it off and chalked it up to Cesar being Cesar.

Samir didn't let Cesar's rants put a damper on his mood. He was excited to hit the road and put his plans in motion. The Corleones loaded up in the car that Samir's step mother rented for them and hit I57 headed south.

While on the outskirts of his city, Samir turned around and looked at the skyline of Chicago. He knew when he returned a week later, everything would be different. He couldn't put his finger on it, but he felt in his soul that their dynamics would soon change.

He looked at his crew and he couldn't have asked for a more loyal bunch. He knew that he was making a good decision with this expansion. What he didn't realize is just how much this expansion was going to change them. They thought they had gone from boys to men up until this point, but this expansion was going to separate the loyal from the fake. His life was about to take a turn and it was one he never imagined. But for now, he just enjoyed the ride.

Eighteen hours later, The Black Corleones arrived in Houston, and the rest of the dope world had a problem.

Chapter Six

Samir woke up early and looked out the window of his Hotel Derek suite that canvassed the view of Houston's Galleria area. He spent most of their ride down thinking of ways he was going to take Houston by storm. He was currently in possession of some of the best dope in the country, and with the work in Houston being cut down to almost nothing, the possibility of a drought down here was highly unlikely. But first he had to meet up with his Houston based crew.

Samir pulled the rest of the Corleones out of bed and they headed over to the Capital Grille to meet with Casey and his crew. Samir was well informed on Casey's reputation. Casey was a young go-getter, like each one of the Corleones. He was making money, but Samir was about to give him the opportunity to be a legend in his prospective city.

Casey was also the top club promoter in H-town;

he knew everybody, so moving the product would be a breeze.

The Corleones walked in the restaurant and Casey was already there waiting for them. Samir appreciated his promptness. It showed just how eager he was to be a part of what the Corleones were doing.

"What's the deal, bro?" Casey greeted Samir.

"What's up, Joe, let me introduce you to my niggas... this is Cesar, Meko, Seven and Chase."

"What's the deal homie," Meko dapped Casey.

"Let's sit down. I took the liberty of ordering some Cristal for our meeting," Casey said.

"That's what's up, what we celebrating though?" Cesar asked.

"We're celebrating taking this game to the next level. We're celebrating this money I'm about to make the Corleones, the money we about to make together. Most importantly, we're celebrating showing these old heads that it's a new generation of hustlers on the horizon," Casey explained.

He was excited to get the opportunity to work with Samir and his crew. He was doing good for himself, but with the Corleones backing him, he knew he was about to be catapulted into the next stratosphere. What the Corleones didn't know was that their reputation exceeded them. They may have never been to Houston, but the city knew who they were before they even arrived.

"Let's get this meeting underway. I'm looking to expand my operation, and I chose you, Casey, because I feel like you got a solid team and you can move the work as efficiently as we do. I have strict guidelines on how shit needs to be run. I will not tolerate money being late. Being that we won't be down here to oversee this operation closely, I'm going to have a tight grip on this until I'm comfortable with your team's ability. I'll pull the plug at the first sign of problems, so if you're sure you want to do this, and be down with us, understand that I'm not going to deal with any fuck ups," Samir explained to Casey.

"I feel you, but let me help you understand something... I ain't get to where I am by being a fuck up. I'm a go getter, and I don't wait for a door to open, I go open them. All I need is the chance. I been doing my thing, but I just didn't have the plug I needed to take over this city. You'll never have to worry about your money, because if y'all give me the opportunity to prove myself, I promise, I'll make y'all multimillionaires before you're twenty. I'm ready. Y'all need this as much as I do, so all I can say is the sooner we get started, the sooner I can prove that this is a good collabo," Casey stood by his position.

"We don't have a doubt that you can handle this, but we need to make sure that us getting in bed with you won't bite us in our ass, because if it does; It won't be nice for you," Meko joined the conversation.

"I understand one hundred percent. Y'all ain't got shit to worry about. This is going to be one hell of an arrangement. That's my word," Casey said in his southern drawl.

"Here's how things are going to go. I'm gon' start you off with twenty kilo's at eight thousand a piece. You have thirty days to get us our money. If you meet the requirement on this first run, my crew and I will determine whether to increase you numbers. So, you got a month to come up with a hundred and sixty thousand. How you sell them, or how much you push them for is your business, but on day thirty one, sixty needs to be paid to us, regardless of your situation."

"That sounds good to me, but to show you how serious I am, that one sixty y'all require, I'm gon' pay that right now," Casey said, handing Samir a Louis Vuitton duffle bag containing two hundred thousand dollars, "That's two hundred right there, take the one sixty for the work and the other forty as a gift from me to you for this chance."

Impressed with the gesture; Samir called Valli so they could start working on Casey's shipment. He felt good about this new partnership. He saw a bit of himself in Casey, and he knew this move was going to be the very thing he was waiting for.

The Corleones spent the rest of their Houston trip learning the city and being introduced to all the movers and shakers of the Houston dope boy scene. He made sure Valli would package the work and have it shipped to Casey before the week was out. With Casey on board, the Corleones were about to become bigger names than they could ever imagine.

On their last night in Houston, Casey invited them out to one of his downtown hot spots, The M bar. He made sure the Corleones were treated like royalty. When they arrived downtown to the club, they were escorted to VIP where their section was already set up for them.

The music was bumping and the groupies where in abundance. Samir and the Corleones were rubbing elbows with some of H-towns elite. Everybody from Houston's top dope boys, to the rappers and ball players, they were all in the building.

The Corleones were surrounded with pretty mixed bitches trying to get chose. Casey sent 10 bottles of premium vodka and champagne to their section. Everybody watched as the sparklers lit up the otherwise dark club. When the bottles arrived to their table, all eyes were on the Corleones. Everybody was wondering who they were. Niggas showed love and the bitches were waiting for a chance to go home with one of them.

"Shout out to my niggas, the Black Corleones are in the fucking place, all the way from the windy city. My niggas celebrating our new business venture. Real niggas do real things!" Casey said over the microphone.

Meko and Seven stood on the couch in their section, bottles in hand and sent Casey a salute. Cesar took a neatly bundled stack of hundred dollar bills and threw them in the air as the VIP area turned-up to the announcement.

Samir sat back and watched his crew enjoy themselves in celebration to their expansion. He tried to relax, but he knew this was just the beginning to the work they were going to have to put in. He wasn't ready to celebrate prematurely, because they still had to lock down New Orleans in the morning, and they still had to have a successful return before he would celebrate anything.

Samir's mind was only on his expansion working, because coming out of the shadow of his family was more important than clubs, popping bottles and hoes. While his crew was enjoying themselves he was already thinking about New Orleans and getting back to Chicago so they could get the ball rolling on this expansion.

Hung over from the night before, Samir and his crew headed to New Orleans to lock down the second part of their deal. Houston was already a go and they needed New Orleans before they could put their kingpin plans into play. After a 3 and half hour drive, they arrived in Baton Rouge to meet with Roland, who would be heading their N.O. operations.

Roland was already doing his thing in New Orleans. He had the entire 9th ward on lock, but he had plans on locking down all of New Orleans, but he could only do that with an alliance through the Corleones.

"Damn, I'm glad y'all were able to come down here. I'm ready to go, homie. I already got my people in line ready to move from here to Slidell. I'm ready to lock down Lousiana, Woo," Roland said as they sat down for lunch.

"We're ready to go to, but before we can do that, we gotta be comfortable in your ability to handle the work load required to meet our standards. You gon' make money, but you gon' be representing our

Corleone name, so we need to make sure you don't make us look bad," Seven explained.

"Trust me when I say, my niggas are monsters in these streets, so if I didn't feel we could handle what the Black Corleones are about, then we would have never put our names in the hat. It's plenty niggas out here that want to be down with y'all, but they ain't half the niggas we are," Roland quickly defended himself.

"I trust in your ability and that's exactly why we're here. So, let me inform you on how this is going to work..." Samir explained the same thing to Roland as he did to Casey. The same rules applied.

"Okay, I understand where you coming from, but I can assure you that you won't regret this decision. I respect you and what you're building. I'm good on my own, but I know with this alliance we'll be great from Louisiana to Chicago," Roland explained.

"Well, be ready because I'm sending everything down here by next week. Your thirty days begins the moment your shipment touches down."

"I got it. Let's make a toast to our new found business venture," Roland said standing to his feet and raising his glass, "I want to make a toast to you niggas for setting the standard for young hustlers like myself, and to our alliance."

Samir finally achieved another level of his dope

career with Roland and Casey joining forces with him and his crew. He knew the next quarter was going to bring in more money than they could count. His plans to expand met him with some nervousness, but he knew at this very moment he no longer had to worry about his ability in this game, because he was built for it. It was in his blood. He was finally Samir, leader of the Black Corleones, and no longer just Carlyle Kendall's son, or Sin and Ace's little brother. He was a boss in his own right.

Chapter Seven

After a successful spring break, the Corleones made it back to Chicago secure about their future in the dope game. Graduation was in less than two months and they had successfully expanded their operation. Samir was feeling like he accomplished everything he set out to do. Valli made sure Casey and Roland were squared away, and the clock was officially set for Roland to prove himself.

Samir sent Casey 25 kilo's because he was impressed by him having the money up front and showing the rest of the Corleones a good time while they were in Houston. The next 30 days would be the test. If they couldn't prove to the co-op that they were capable of handling sets outside of Chicago, then the plan of expansion would become null and void.

Samir was feeling confident with all that was going on around him when he decided to check in on his sets.

"How did everything go with the shipments?" Samir asked Valli

"It went well. I just got word that everything was received, so it's a go. I got the numbers for this month as well," Valli said

"Oh yeah, how did you do, Joe?"

"Four point five million, we pulled in four point five million dollars."

"You got to be shitting me?" Samir said in shock.

"No my nigga, that shit is real. We squared away on all aspects. We've been moving heavy around here, and we gon' need to re-up soon," Valli laughed.

The news put Samir on a high he hadn't felt since they passed his father's test with flying colors. He couldn't wait to share the news with his crew. Four and a half million dollars in a month was definitely a milestone for the Corleones.

Meanwhile, on the other side of town, Carlyle Kendall was also hearing of his son's four million dollar month.

"Carlyle, you know we have your best interest at heart, but there's nothing we can do here, our hands are tied here. Your son is bringing to much attention to himself. I know they're trying to stay under wraps, but it looks really suspicious for a group of eighteen year olds to be pulling in four million dollars," DEA Agent Ken Fitzgerald informed Carlyle.

"Am I not paying you guys very handsomely, so, telling me your hands are tied isn't going to fly with me, and you know me well enough to know that; this is my son here, and he's not ready to be raided, or to even have these problems right now. I haven't equipped him to deal with y'all yet. He's not ready," Carlyle expressed.

"Well, Carlyle, when he clocked in four and a half million dollars, he became ready to deal with every aspect of his career choice. We don't want to bring heat to your son or your operation. We came down here because we have respect for you and wanted to let you know what was about to go down so you can equipped your son," Agent Keith Simpson chimed in.

"Explain to me how y'all even get wind of my son if he is keeping himself out of the light?" Carlyle asked the agents.

"To be honest with you, your son and his crew are rubbing some of the other crews the wrong way with the way they're moving. They're becoming the top suppliers and not leaving much room for anybody else. There have been a few tips on your boy for some months now, so much so, that the word came down the wire to send in a raid to see if the reports are true," Agent Fitzgerald explained.

"When's this raid going to happen?"

"It's going to happen this upcoming Wednesday, and it'll be simultaneous with all his spots."

"Okay, well, thank you guys for coming over and informing me," Carlyle told him as he escorted the agents out of his home.

"Carlyle, just make sure we don't find anything. It's time to acclimate Samir to the process and get him a few people on his payroll, because he can't always rely on daddy," Agent Simpson said as they departed.

Carlyle knew that eventually he would have to train the young Corleones to every aspect of the game, and that included having a payoff budget for law enforcement, but he figured he had a little more time. He wasn't expecting them to make the kind of money they were making, and especially not in a month's time. He made the decision right then to slow them down, because protecting his son was far more important than any dollar amount.

"Are you okay, Lyle?" Tim asked.

"Yea, I'm straight. I'm just not ready for this right now. Samir is not ready to have to deal with the laws."

"Samir can handle this Lyle, trust me. The boy

just did something we didn't even do when we started out. He's built for this; he can handle it."

"I hope so. Get them over here right now, the entire crew. We gotta inform them on what's about to happen so they can be ready."

"Don't worry Lyle, I got you," Tim assured him.

Samir you and the rest of the Corleones need to get to your father's now!!! Tim messaged Samir.

What's up, is everything ok with my dad?" Samir responded.

"Your pops is good. Y'all just get y'all asses to his house ASAP. All of y'all Samir."

Samir stared at his two-way, anxious and a bit nervous about what this could be about. He forwarded the message to the rest of the Corleones and was ensured that they were on their way to his father's house.

"Yo, I gotta get to my father's house bro, make sure everybody gets paid, and let me know how much we need to re-up on," Samir instructed Valli.

"I got you kid. I'll have that for you by the end of the day."

Samir jumped in his car and drove full speed

toward his dad's house. He was worried about the urgency of this meeting. He couldn't help but let his mind's worries consume him. He replayed the last few days in his head, trying to come up with a reason his father would call a meeting so sudden.

As he pulled up to the house, he saw Meko and Seven walking in, and then Chase pulled up behind him. Cesar was nowhere in sight, but Samir couldn't worry about Cesar at this point, because he was more concerned with the reason for them being here.

"Dad, is everything okay?" Samir asked his father as they filed into the basement.

"Everything is fine with me. Where's Cesar, Sam?" Carlyle asked.

"I don't know. I hit him and told him we had to be here."

"How long has he been M.I.A?

"A little while,"

"Shit like this is exactly why I didn't want you to pull him into your ranks. The fact that he didn't show up when I specifically said for all of you to be here means that he doesn't respect you. And when niggas don't respect you, they'll do anything to you. You make sure you watch him, Samir... because I'm starting to sense a snake in the grass."

"Don't worry about that Mr. Kendall, I got that

handled," Meko chimed in.

Samir looked at Meko in shock. He had no idea he was watching Cesar, but after Cesar's little outburst during their spring break trip, Meko no longer trusted him and kept a close eye on him for the sake of the family.

"So, Mr. Kendall... what was so important we had to come over so quickly?" Seven asked.

"Well, first let me congratulate you guys on a four million dollar month. That's no easy feat, and I'm damn proud of all of you, but we have a little problem," Carlyle explained to them.

"Wait, Mr. Kendall, how can making four million dollars in a month be a problem?" Chase added.

"Yea pops, he's right. What's the problem in making money?" Samir asked.

"The fact that y'all made four million dollars in a month is the problem. I was just informed from few of my agents that you guys are about to be raided by the DEA. A few people haven't liked what y'all been doing out here and leaked reports to the feds and now they have *just cause* to come at you guys. And frankly, you cannot afford any fuck ups at this point, and you're most certainly not ready to deal with this aspect of the game."

"What are you saying pops?" Samir asked him.

"What I'm saying is; I have to protect you

because you are my son. So, first thing y'all gon' do is make sure they find nothing in your spots. Everything needs to be moved. When they show up, you and your people are to cooperate fully with their investigation. None of you will be anywhere near those spots during the raids. Last, it's time for you guys to have a payoff budget, because despite how y'all been wanting to stay low key, the fact of the matter is, you guys are not under the radar anymore," he explained.

"When is this raid supposed to go down, Mr. Kendall? Meko asked.

"Wednesday, so that gives y'all two days to make sure there's no evidence of your operation in none of those spots. It needs to be so clean over there that it puts the feds off of your trail. Next, I'm cutting y'all way down until this shit blows over. Y'all are going through too much work in too short of a time frame," Carlyle explained.

"Cut us down... pops, I can't afford to be cut, we moving too much work, and we just expanded our operation down south," Samir pleaded.

"Samir, I don't have a choice. This is too much right now, and you guys are going to be under scrutiny after this raid. The heat is on, and I have to do what's best for y'all, and for our operation. I gotta cut y'all from seventy five to a hundred kilos to about twenty five to fifty kilos, max, until this shit blows over."

"Twenty five kilo's? Dad, what are we gonna do with twenty five kilo's? We ship that much out of town. We can't cover Chicago, our out of town customers, and our expansion off that."

"Look, Samir, I guess you're gonna have to get back to the way you were when you when you were trying to pass your test to get in the game. My decision is final. I'm cutting you down until the heat is off. It's for the best, trust me. Besides, y'all just made damn near five million dollars; I think y'all can relax."

"Relax, we can't relax pops. You of all people know if we let up somebody will snatch our spot. You're only relevant as your last re-up. If I can't supply my customers, what's going to make them not go cop from somebody else?" Samir said.

"Wow, I really thought y'all had it figured out, but now I know y'all got so much to learn. Let me explain something to y'all, it's not about how much money you make, how much work you move, or how large your clientele is. The secret to this game is how many of those niggas remain loyal to you as their supplier. This game is about building the type of organization where niggas think twice about fucking with somebody else. It's about being the type of niggas that people respect, and will remain loyal to, no matter what the situation. If you focus on that, niggas will never wanna cop from anybody but you, because they're loyal. You youngsters need to redirect your focus from money to loyalty, and once you gain that, you'll never have to worry about making money again, because niggas are going to make sure y'all always got a steady flow," Carlyle schooled the young Corleones.

"That's real Mr. Kendall. I got it. I think we all got it," Seven said on the behalf of his entire crew."

"I'm not saying that this will last long, just until the heat dies down. We just gotta make sure these boys back all the way off. Right now just focus on getting things squared away for Wednesday," Carlyle told them.

After their meeting with Carlyle, the Corleones headed out to start clearing their spots. Carlyle called Samir back downstairs because he was more than concerned about Cesar. He wanted to make sure that Samir kept a good grip on this situation before it got out of hand.

"Samir what the fuck is going on with Cesar?"

"I don't know what's been going on with him lately, but I ain't worried about it," Samir defended his friend.

"That's the problem, son, I think you need to

worry. How the fuck he not show up to a meeting that required all of you. I don't like that shit, Sam. I take it as a sign of disrespect to you, and most importantly, to me," Carlyle explained.

"Pops, I'm sure there's a good explanation for his absence, but don't trip. I'll handle Cesar," Samir told his father. He didn't want him to know how Cesar had been acting, because he knew he would take matters into his own hands. Cesar was still his man and haven't given him any real cause to doubt him, but now with his father questioning him and Meko on the defense, he knew he had to talk to Cesar sooner or later.

Samir left his father's house, but he wasn't worried about the raid, he was more concerned with figuring out where Cesar stood, because his absence was deafening.

"What up Joe." Samir messaged Cesar. But the message went unanswered. He took the long way to his condo, constantly looking down at his two-way, hoping Cesar would respond. The more he waited, the more agitated he became. He tried not to listen to his father's voice, but the truth was; it was getting to him. As he was about to pick up his phone to call Cesar, it rang with a number he didn't recognized.

"Yo, state your case," he angrily answered.

"Hello, Samir, it's me," a sweet, but sad voice was on the other end of the phone.

"Khloe, baby, is that you?"

"Yes, it's me, are you busy?" she said crying into the receiver.

"Khloe, what's wrong baby, where are you?"

"I'm at a payphone. Can you come and get me, please? I can't take her beating me for nothing, please come, please..."

"A payphone, what the fuck you mean? Where's the phone I brought you, and where are you exactly?"

"She found it and took it away. I'm in Country Club Hills at the Walgreens on One Eighty Third and Pulaski. Can you please come, please?"

"Khlo, just hold tight, I'm on my way. Don't worry, and don't move. I'm coming baby girl," he told her as he turned around and headed in her direction.

Samir did 100 on the express way to get to her. He jumped in and out lanes, praying she was okay, and that he didn't get pulled over. He didn't care about the danger of his reckless driving; he had to get to her.

When he pulled up, he saw her standing outside, alone next to the payphone. He jumped out of his car before he could put it in park, took his Avirex velour jacket off, and put it around her as he hugged her and wiped her tears. Samir kissed her forehead and assured her that everything would be okay, because she was with him now.

"Khloe, I promise, you're safe with me. You never have to go back, okay. I'll always take care of you," he told her, kissing her hand.

"Thank you for coming," she told him, with tears in her eyes.

"You don't have to thank me. I love you, and I will always be here for you. I don't want you to worry about nothing. I got you," he told her.

"Wait, did you just say you love me?" Khloe asked him in shock.

"Yes Khloe, I love you. I've always loved you. From the first day I saw you."

She didn't speak for a moment because she was shocked to hear someone actually say they loved her. It was a phrase she had longed for her whole life, and here he was, the least likely person, telling her he loved her.

"Samir, I love you too, but there is something I need to tell you."

"Don't worry about it, baby girl. It doesn't even matter because I already know how old you are."

"How did you know that's what I was going to say?"

"I just had a feeling."

Samir held her hand the whole ride to his condo. He glanced at her as she stared out the window, wondering what was on her mind. He knew she had been through a lot of turmoil in her young life, but she was with him, and it's exactly where he always wanted her to be.

Samir knew he couldn't change what she already went through, but he would make sure her future was brighter than her past.

Khloe stared at the bright lights as they drove through the streets of downtown, and for the first time, she could breathe. She didn't know how the rest of her life would play out, but she knew as long as she was with Samir, she was safe.

As they pulled up to his building, she looked at the high rise in awe. She had never been anywhere as beautiful.

"Is this where you live?" she asked.

"Yea, this is my place."

"You live here with your mother or something?"

"Naw baby, my momma don't live here. It's just you and me," he laughed.

Her eyes widened as the door man welcomed Samir back home. The majesty of the foyer was breathtaking, and right then she realized he wasn't just some small time corner hustler. Looking at the décor of the building, Khloe realized Samir was bigger in the game then he let on.

When they arrived in front of apartment 1507, he handed her the keys, kissed her cheek and welcomed her home to her new life.

She walked into the condo and was taking back by how luxurious it was. The neo Italian furniture, marble counters, and back splashes were something she only seen on television or in magazines.

Khloe took her shoes off to see if the carpet felt as soft as it looked. Then she saw the sparkle of the moon on Lake Michigan from his living room window. The view of the city was more stunning than she ever imagined. She started crying because she couldn't believe he had finally saved her from her misery, and gave her something wonderful.

"What's the matter, baby girl?" he asked, as he stood behind her and put his arms around her.

"It's just so pretty down here. Your house is so beautiful,"

"Well, it's your house now. It's ours. You believe I'll take care of you, right?"

"I don't know Samir, to be honest with you."

"Listen to me Khloe, I swear on my life, I will always take care of you. You're safe now. I just want you to smile, because you can be happy knowing that I will always be here, okay."

Just as she was about to answer him, his two-way went off with a message from Cesar. Samir didn't return the message. He called and set up a meeting with Cesar right then and there. He couldn't put it off any longer, especially with the raid coming down the pipeline.

He kissed Khloe on the forehead and snapped back into hustler mode. He made sure she was comfortable, and headed out to meet with Cesar.

When Samir arrived at Cesar's house, he noticed a few cars he didn't recognize, but he didn't pay it any mind. He called inside for Cesar to come out because he didn't want to speak business around niggas he didn't know.

"What's the deal, Ces?" Samir greeted him when he came out.

"What's good, bro?" Cesar dapped him.

"Let's take a ride my nigga, cuz' it's some things we need to discuss."

"What's on your mind, bro?" Cesar asked, as they drove through the wild 100's.

"You tell me, my nigga. You been acting real fucked up lately, Joe. First, that shit you pulled when we were going to Houston, and then you didn't show up today when I specifically told all you niggas to be at my pops house. I'm starting to feel like you don't respect me or what we trying to build," Samir told him.

"First off, I said what I had to say on the day we were leaving for H-town, so I'm not gonna get back into that. And as far as going to your pops house, I didn't think I needed to be there, plus, I had some other shit to do anyway."

"What the fuck you mean you had some other shit to do. I told you we needed to be there, so that other shit should've been dropped. You made me look like an ass in front of my pops, my nigga. Now is your chance to start being a hunit, my nigga. If you don't want to be a part of this family; then speak up now. We've been through too much together for one nigga to bring down what we been working towards, and besides, my pops informed us that we about to be raided, so yea, you needed to fucking be there, my nigga. This ego shit you got going on needs to stop right fucking now."

"I'm not the one with the ego, bro. I didn't show up to the meeting because I felt like you didn't need me. I'm supposed to be your right hand, second in command, and you treat me like I'm a worker. I'm supposed to be at the co-op meetings with you, instead, you took Meko. I've been down since we were little kids, and this nigga Meko closer to you than I am," Cesar tried to play on Samir's emotions, but deep down he didn't care about being second in command, he wanted to be the top guy, because he was tired of living in Samir's shadow. Money was changing Cesar and turning him into the apple that didn't fall far from the tree.

"My nigga, we started this thing together, the five of us. Meko went to the meetings with me because my father requested it. He's the leader of this co-op and we have to do what he says, because he made all of this shit possible. He gave us this chance, and I respect my pops. You made me look weak, like I didn't have a handle on my shit. How you wanna be second in command if you always under minding me and being difficult? Shit like that makes us look like we don't have unity in our crew. And it has everything to do with ego. You so worried about titles, that you missing the bigger picture, my nigga. We out here doing shit that ain't never been done by niggas our age since them Harlem niggas did it in the eighties."

"My ego ain't got nothing to do with shit," Cesar interrupting him.

"Nigga, stop interrupting me, Joe... and listen to what I'm trying to tell you. We a fucking family and we need to move like one. That meeting wasn't optional, bro. You so busy worrying about dumb shit, you don't even know we made four and a half million dollars this past month. Niggas is starting to do bogus shit; like report us to the feds. My pops called all of us in to inform us that we're being raided on Wednesday. But you wouldn't know that cuz' you acting like a female. Jealous over some Meko shit. Nigga, we're the Black Corleones, there is no one man above this family."

"Damn, *a raid?* I had no idea, Sam. I been tripping, bro. My bad, I should've been there. I'm down with this family, and I'll work on my shit, but what we gon' do about this raid?"

"Nothing we can do about it. We just gotta let it happen; but we gon' clean out our traps and move everything. Pops is cutting us down until things smooth over. We really gotta put in work to cover our shorts until the heat is off. Then we need to set aside a payoff budget. Shit getting real out here, Ces, and I need all y'all down with me to continue what we started."

"I got you, bro."

"We need to be at the spots in the morning, before class so we can make sure shit gets squared away before Wednesday."

Samir dropped Cesar off back at his house. He was hoping he got through to him because they couldn't afford to have any more hang ups, especially with the alphabet boys on their heels.

When he got back to his building, it was the first time he was excited about being home, because despite everything he was dealing with in the streets and with the game, he knew Khloe was inside waiting for him. He had a reason to leave the woes of his hustler life at the door.

When he walked into his condo there she was, asleep on the couch, looking like an angel in his eyes. He walked over and kissed her forehead, unintentionally waking her up.

"Hey, Khloe, why are you on the couch, babes?" he asked.

"I fell asleep waiting for you to come home."

"Well, I'm here now, so let's go to bed."

That night he slept peacefully with Khloe in his arms. She couldn't have come to him at a better time, because he was going to need some serenity with all that was about to happen in the streets.

Chapter Eight

Samir sat in fourth period with his stomach in knots. He was praying to God that the feds didn't find anything tied to his operation. He couldn't focus on his class because the nervousness was making him sick, literally.

He checked his phone and pager ever two minutes, hoping for a word that it was all over. Wednesday morning came too quick for his taste. He didn't get in the game to have these kinds of problems, and he was naive to think that they would stay under the radar of the laws.

But Samir wasn't the only Corleone nervous about that morning. Meko and Seven sat in the back of their class on pins and needles. They knew they emptied their spots completely, but they couldn't help to wonder how things were unfolding.

Cesar and Chase headed to lunch off campus, and although they wanted to ride by their spots, they knew it would be best if all members of the Corleone family stayed as far away from the trap as possible.

While the Corleones where sweating bricks, the DEA raid teams were in position to simultaneously hit all four of the Black Corleone's trap spots.

After suiting up, Agent Carl Scott lead his team to hit the Corleone's Gardens spot. Agent Scott gave a silent count down and his agents took their ram straight through the door of the apartment.

"Everybody get down on the ground, now!" Agent Scott shouted as they gained entry.

Valli, his girl and a few of Samir's workers were in the apartment, but they were fully briefed on the raid that was going to happen. He made sure the place was as clean as a whistle, so no one was the least bit nervous. They cooperated as agents filled the apartment.

"No disrespect sir, but do you have a warrant for breaking my door?" Valli asked, as the agents began to tear up the apartment apart.

"Get the fuck on the ground like I told you, and don't ask me shit," Agent Scott said.

Agent Scott took his job serious, and was one of few agents who didn't allow himself to be turned. With promotions coming up, he needed this bust to be successful. Agents on Carlyle's payroll were placed on Samir's other trap spots and couldn't oversee the dealings of Agent Scott's raid detail.

After 30 minutes of searching the house, Agent Scott was furious that he came up empty handed. He had all the people in the house ran through the system for warrants, but Valli and his crew was clean.

He gave a call to the agents in charge of the other raids, and they all reported that they also came up with nothing.

Agent Scott felt like something was amiss. He wondered how all four houses came up empty when they had so many tips coming in about the Black Corleones operation.

"We didn't find anything, sir. But I believe we're on the right track. I would like permission to continue investigations," Agent Scott reported to his commanding officer.

"I'm sorry, Scott, we got bigger fish to fry in this city and we can't waist any more time on this. It's just rumors at this point," his supervisor responded.

"But sir, we—" Agent Scott began to speak before he was cut off.

"—No buts, Scott, you hit every location and came up with nothing. No drugs, guns or money, and not to mention the people in the houses were clean as whistles. This investigation is over. Get back to the office to be briefed on your next assignment. This horse is dead."

And with that, the Black Corleones had dodged their first bullet with law enforcement.

Meanwhile, Carlyle was headed downtown with Tim when his DEA informant gave him the call that everything was clear and Samir and his crew dodged their first bullet with the feds. He was relieved that the youngsters were as thorough as they were, but he was still firm on cutting them down until the heat was completely off of them. He was proud of his young crew and decided not to cut them down as much as he originally planned.

"Tim, hit my boy and let him know that he can resume business as usual," Carlyle requested.

"I got you, Lyle."

Samir was in his last period of the day. His nerves on edge when he received the message from Tim informing him that his business could return to normal, relieved, he took a deep breath and got back into a hustler's state of mind.

Just know that we still cutting you guys down as a precaution but your pops has decided to forgo the extreme cut. We will let you know what you get by the end of the week. Tim informed Sam.

Samir didn't respond, he just decided to let the rest of his crew know they were back in business. He felt his nerves settle. The last few days leading up to the raid had him on edge. This was the last thing they needed with the expansion. He knew news was traveling fast, so he was a bit worried that his clientele would want to fall back, because nobody wants to fuck with niggas who had the feds sniffing around their operation. But what Samir didn't know was the raid would only make The Black Corleones more popular amongst the rest of the dope world.

The streets were pumping about how the youngest team in the Chi left the feds empty handed. While the hood was praising Samir and his crew, Cesar didn't like what he was hearing.

Walking to his car after class, he overheard a few corner hustlers from around the way talking about how Samir was the man, and how he had the feds dumbfounded when his spots came up empty. Cesar was furious hearing Samir getting all the credit when he felt he was doing all the work. In his mind, Samir wasn't half the man he was; and he didn't understand why the fuck everybody was always speaking so highly of him, like he was the one doing all the grinding.

Even though Samir and the rest of the Corleones didn't care about titles and recognition, it was the only thing Cesar cared about. His focus had shifting in the short time they were climbing to the top.

The money they were making was beginning to change Cesar. He had always had love for Samir since his childhood, but in the same token he wasn't in the position he was in now. He didn't credit Samir for helping them get there, and he refused to own up to the fact that it was Samir's alliance that put them in this position. All he cared about was niggas saying Samir's name more than his own.

Being in a crew was starting to bother Cesar and he began to devise a plan to set out on his own. He wanted to be a leader, but he didn't realize that he didn't have leadership characteristics. He wanted to be done with this Corleone bullshit, but he knew that right now wasn't the time to break away, not with all the money they were about to make with their expansion. He knew he had to try his best not to let his envy show, but he couldn't help but to be who he had always been preconceived to be.

Chapter Nine

A few months passed since the Corleones first run-in with the feds. Business for them tripled when news got out that they were a thorough young crew who could be trusted. Their expansion down south had been more than a good decision for the youngsters; in fact, it was the best decision they ever made since coming into their own.

Their profit margins tripled since they joined the game, and life couldn't be better. Not only were they making money, but they had finally reached graduation day, and with this school bullshit behind them, they no longer had any restraints occupying their time.

Graduation day was huge for the crew, and they had the biggest graduation party in the city. Anybody who was somebody showed up to party with Chicago's brightest hood stars.

Dressed in a black Armani tux, Samir looked at

himself in the mirror before he put on his cap and gown and finally felt the pride he should have felt from day one. He achieved what he set out to do, and today was more than him graduating from high school; today was about him graduating from the shadows of the Kendall family name, and building his own.

As he stood there, his mood became somber for a moment, because although today was a joyous occasion, he couldn't help but to think about Sin and Ace, and how their absence was taking a toll on him. He was achieving something major in his reign, and he couldn't share it with them. He wanted so much for his brothers to be by his side; that he couldn't truly be happy knowing they weren't there.

"Baby, what's wrong?" Khloe asked from the doorway of their bedroom.

"Nothing's wrong. I'm okay," he said as he turned to face her. He couldn't help but to stare at her. She looked like an angel dressed in a white Alexander McQueen dress and crystal Guiseppe's, "Nothing is ever wrong when you're around," he said, kissing her forehead.

"Okay, baby. Your mother called and said to hurry up because they want to take pictures before we go to the graduation."

"I'm ready. You look beautiful by the way. How did a hood nigga like me get so lucky to have you; I'll never understand," he kissed her forehead.

On the way to his father's house, Khloe's nerves were on edge. This was the first time she was meeting his family since she came to live with him a few months earlier. She knew he told his family about her, but she was worried that they would judge her and their relationship being that she was no older than his younger sister. Khloe was worried if she would fit in with their family dynamics. She knew how much they meant to him, and she just wanted to make a good impression.

"I don't know about this, Samir," Khloe expressed as they pulled in front of his father's house.

"Don't know about what?" he replied.

"Going in that house with you as your girl, what if they hate me?"

"Why would they hate you, baby, I love you, so my family is going to love you too," he smiled as he kissed her fears away.

He helped her out of the car and he could feel her nerves radiating, so he held her hand tighter and lead her inside the house.

Her palms began to sweat and she felt a lump in her throat as she watched Samir call out to his family. All at once, they rushed to him, excited that today was his big day. His mother hugged him with tears in her eyes. She was grateful that he kept his promise, but she was also in silent agony that her older boys weren't going to see him accept his diploma. His father hugged him in a way a man hugs his son, and his sister joked about him being old.

Khloe stood there, watching how his family reacted. It made her sad because she never felt that before. She never knew what it was like to feel love from her mother, and be a daddy's little girl, like his sister. She tried hold in her tears, so she swallowed hard as he introduced her to everyone.

To her surprise, every one of the Kendall's welcomed her with open arms. His stepmother was in awe of how beautiful she was, and his sister was happy there was another girl she could talk to. They made her feel like she was already a part of their family, and for the first time in her life, she felt like she belonged somewhere, and to somebody. At that moment she fell deeper in love with Samir because he had given her something she always wanted, and that was a family.

Samir's excitement for his graduation day grew more intense as he watched his family accept Khloe with open arms; no questions asked. He watched her chat with his sister and hoped she was finally experiencing the happiness he had promised her from the very beginning.

His trance was broken by the ringing of his father's door bell. When he opened the door, the rest of his crew was standing there, all dressed to the nines with caps and gowns in hand. Even Cesar appeared to be genuinely happy for the occasion as they all greeted each other.

Their stretch Hummer limo pulled up just in time to escort them to the graduation venue in style.

Samir introduced Khloe to the rest of the Black Corleones and she was more nervous meeting them than she was meeting his family.

"Yo, fam, is that shorty from Harolds you met a while back?" Meko inquired.

"Yea, that's my baby," Samir boasted with pride.

"Yea, she's more beautiful than I remember her, Joe," Seven complimented.

"Where her friends at, Joe?" Chase asked.

"She only got one, but I think she fucking with one of them low end niggas," Samir told him.

After some small talk the fellas jumped into the limo and headed to their graduation. This was one of the best days of their young lives because all they could think of was the amount of money they were going to make without the added distraction of school. They could now focus on making their Black Corleone brand bigger and better. The focus was only on their business and nothing else. No parents in their ears begging them to finish school, no cutting their nights short due to early morning classes, and no more having to hear their parents telling them to focus on school. Samir's only focus from this point on was his organization; and making more money than any group of young boys in their city ever did.

But today, Samir wasn't worried about the business; his only concern was walking across the stage and bringing the entire city out for their graduation party. Everybody was talking about it. The Black Corleone's party was going to be the only party that day. The bar was covered, the door was free, and every senior graduating that day would be there. All the females were trying to catch the eye of one of the Corleones, or any big money nigga that was going to be there.

"Make sure y'all get to Secrets tonight for the biggest graduation party in the city. Samir, Meko, Cesar, Chase and Seven are walking across the stage this afternoon, and tonight they are bringing the city out to celebrate. The door is free all night for graduating seniors. The bar is paid

for all night. This is going to be the biggest graduating event the city has seen. You don't want to miss Secret tonight!" the radio DJ announced just in time to amp the Corleones for their graduation.

Sam, I'll be there in time for your grad party, G. Oh, and I got something for you, so we gon' party hard tonight cuz' the last few months been good to me fucking with you boys. Casey messaged Samir as they pulled up to their graduation venue.

"Casey is on his way and he said he got something for us," Samir informed the rest of the crew.

"You know what that means coming from Casey," Meko joked.

"He got that money bag for us. That nigga ain't fucking around."

"Let's not focus on business right now, let's just hit this graduation so we can go eat, cuz' I'm hungry as fuck," Cesar interrupted.

"We ain't focused on business, I'm just letting y'all know Casey and his crew on the way and F.Y.I, our shit never sleeps," Samir replied as they filed out of the car.

Their families where already waiting for them in the parking lot. Khloe rode with Samir's little sister at her request.

"Damn, I missed you little lady," Samir said, hugging Khloe like he hadn't seen her in months.

"Awww, come on lover boy, we gotta take a couple of flicks before we separate from our fams," Chase teased.

"This nigga is straight whipped," Meko joked as he put his arm around Samir's neck, pulling him away from Khloe. "Girl, what you doing to my boy, you got him out her simpin'."

"Screw you niggas. I'm not whipped, but my girl brings a soft side out of me. A nigga need that in this world we in."

They took what seemed like a million pictures with their families before heading inside to join their senior class. Samir and his crew where like hood celebrities in their school.

As they walked in they were stopped by all the popular girls for hugs and daps by every nigga who thought they were somebody in school. Some of their teachers and school staff watched in disgust because they assumed the worst. They didn't think most of the students would amount to much.

Most of them had a preconceived notion that the girls would end up young mothers on welfare, and the boys would end up dead or in jail. But for Samir and the Corleones, today was about the next chapter in their lives, and today was only about celebrating how far they had come, and how far they were about to go.

The students lined up and marched to their seats as the crowd cheered them on. The graduation proceedings were under way, but none of the Corleones were remotely interested in the speech from the principal or the valedictorian. They just wanted to grab their diplomas and get on with the rest of their dope boy lives.

After some ongoing speeches, the moment they had been waiting for, for the past four years had finally arrived. One by one, each of the Corleones walked across the stage, eager for the next step in their life. Samir stood in line and looked into the crowd where he spotted his family, and his heart. He focused on them while he waited his turn. With one student in front of him, Samir's happiness dwindled when reality set in that there were two very important faces missing in his cheering section. He was graduating and his brothers weren't there. One of the biggest moments of his life, and he couldn't share it with his idols. Sin and Ace's absent hadn't hit him as hard until this very moment.

"Graduating with honors and a three point nine grade average, Samir Kendall," The principal called his name.

Samir walked across the stage and tears began to flow as he heard his whole family screaming his name and cheering for him, but he couldn't hear Sin and Ace's voice. He looked his principal in the eyes and shook his hand as he took his high school diploma. He held his diploma up in the air as he walked across the stage, sending his family into frenzy.

This is for my brothers. I did it bro. He said to himself.

After two hours of proceedings, their graduation had come to an end, and with the principals announcement of the graduating class, The Corleones found each other in the crowd and threw their caps in the air as they hugged each other and posed for pictures.

These were the moments Samir lived for. Having his boys by his side and accomplishing everything he set out to do. He looked at his crew and his loyalty to them grew in that moment. He would happily go to his grave with them, and for them. Without them, he was nothing. Tonight was their night, and he would make sure it was a night they would remember.

Chapter Ten

After graduation, the Corleones and their families met at Landry's for a private post-graduation dinner before their party. Carlyle invited everyone to dinner which he happily paid for. It was the first time he was in the same room with Cesar's family since his falling out with Cesar's father. It vexed him to be in the same vicinity with Zeek, but he tried to not let it ruin his son's moment.

Zeek and Carlyle started in the game together along with Tim, and he trusted him like Samir trusted Cesar, but after money came into play, Zeek began to show his true colors. Carlyle and Tim built a fast empire, and when news came that Zeek was going behind their back, trying to strike a deal of his own, Carlyle shut him down, and put word out they he could never do business in Chicago again.

His real intention was to snuff Zeek, because in his line a work, if you don't cut your grass low, the snake in the grass would come back and bite you in the ass. But Carlyle didn't feel right taking a father from his unborn child; so instead, he cut off any possibility of Zeek making money in his city. But he made sure he kept close eyes on him throughout the years, especially since their sons remained friends.

Carlyle sat back and watched his son interact with his crew. He was instantly taken back to his youth. He saw so much of himself in Samir, and didn't realize that he would see such a similar version of himself in his youngest son. He always thought Sin would be the one more like him, but watching Samir's rise in the game changed his view on who would be his true successor.

He was proud of his son, and watching his first steps into manhood made him feel confident in his job as a father. It was his son's night and he had a few surprises in store for Samir and the Corleones. He wanted to make sure it was a night to remember for his boys, and for all of the graduating seniors that were planning to attend.

"Samir, are you happy you're finally done with school?" his sister asked him as they ordered their food.

"Yea, I am sissy. You're next." Carlyle stood up and brought the room to attention for a toast. This was the moment Carlyle could let his guard down and admit he was wrong about not wanting Samir to join the business. He stood in front of the Corleones and their families and held up his glass.

"I want to make a toast to my son, Meko, Seven, Chase and Cesar. Congratulations on graduating high school when most young men your age chose not to. I can't express to the five of you how proud I am of what you've become in the last couple of years. This crew has become more than my son's childhood friends, you're like my sons as much as the ones I created. Being able to be a part of your lives has enriched mines so much. Watching you makes me think of the all the times Tim and I had when we were your age. Now that the next chapter of your lives is about to begin, my only wish is that you keep the bond you created, and that you remain loyal to each other... to my baby boy and his crew," he raised his glass in the air.

"To Samir and his crew," the rest of the room followed suit.

Samir and his crew stood up and thanked everyone in the room. He gave a special thanks to his father for allowing him to be the kind of man he wanted to be, but his extreme gratitude was toward his mother. The last few years had been hard for her with her sons being locked up and her youngest joining the family business. He wanted to make sure she knew how much he loved her, and how much he appreciated having such an amazing and understanding mother by his side.

He presented her with a box that held a model toy Lexus truck that she had been wanting, but when she opened the box the key to the truck fell out. With tears in her eyes, she hugged Samir tighter than she ever hugged anyone.

"That's not all mom," he said, as he presented another box; this time holding a presidential Rolex watch with a diamond bezel. He knew he could never repay his mother for all she had done for him and his brothers, but at least he could try.

After dinner, the Corleones said goodbye to their families and headed to Samir's place to get ready for their party.

"So, how was the ride with my sister and parents?" he asked, as they walked to his car.

"It was fun. Your sister is really cool, and your step mother is funny as hell."

"Well, I'm glad you were okay and felt comfortable. My family already loves you, and my mother swears you look like the daughter she always wanted. I got something for you though."

"Boy, you didn't need to buy me nothing, but what is it?" she laughed.

"I'll show you when we get back home."

As they pulled up in front of her friend Shay's house, she saw her standing outside, arguing with her boyfriend. Khloe jumped out the car as fast as she could to calm her friend down. She tried to pull Shay inside, but he wouldn't let them past. Samir watched from his car and he heard Shay's man call her and Khloe *'dirty little bitches'* Before he could think about it, he jumped out of his car in full attack mode.

"Say, my nigga, what the fuck you just call my girl?" he questioned as he approached the dude who had his back turned.

Shay's boyfriend was about to jump fly when he recognized Samir's face, "Oh, I didn't mean no disrespect, Corleone. I swear I didn't know this was your girl, Joe," he immediately corrected himself.

"You don't mean no disrespect? Why nigga, cuz' you know who the fuck I am. But just a second ago you were real disrespectful."

"Naw fam, I didn't mean nothing. Me and my girl just having a little disagreement, you know how that go."

"No, I don't know how that go, cuz' I wasn't raised to disrespect women. I tell you what; Shay's going with me and my girl tonight. If I catch you around her again, it's not gon' be nice."

"Listen, this is my girl, bro and this is our

business. I fuck with you Corleone niggas, and I make y'all a lot of money. I'm asking that you let me handle my own shit."

"Nigga, who the fuck are you and don't mention no fucking money to me again. I'm gon' ask you one more time to get the fuck away from this crib."

"Aight Sam... I'm out. Shay, lose my number," he said as he walked away.

"Oh my God, thank you so much Samir. I been trying to get rid of that nigga ever since he got his other bitch pregnant; Khloe, girl, what's up?" Shay said in relief.

"Girl, are you ready, cuz' you know how long it's gonna take you to get dressed when we get to my house," Khloe said trying to not think about what just happened. But she couldn't help but to let her mind wonder about how big Samir really was in the streets. From the way Shay's boyfriend reacted, Samir's reputation exceeded its self far more than he let on.

Khloe didn't say much on their way to the house, and Samir could sense she was a little uneasy. By the time they made it back to their condo, Samir's phone and two-way was blowing up from people asking where they were. They were telling him that the club was bananas.

While Khloe was getting dressed, Samir walked

into the room with the gift he told her about on their way to Shay's house. She opened it and found a green box with the word Rolex etched in gold. When she opened the case, her eyes widened at the sight of her gold presidential Rolex watch. She had never had such an expensive gift in her life. As she began to speak, Samir quickly interrupted her.

"I know Khlo, you don't have to say nothing. I know I didn't have to, but I wanted to. I'd give you the world if I could. Just tell me you like it."

"I love it, and I love you, Samir."

"I love you too," he removed the watch from the box, and just as he was about to place it on her wrist, he turned it around so she could see the inscription which read *I'll Love You Always Khlo. SC.* She felt her eyes begin to water, but she had to shake it off because she didn't want to mess up her make-up. She kissed him more passionately than she ever kissed him before. She felt her lower region tingle. He attempted to mount her and she instantly got nervous and stopped him.

"What's wrong?" he asked her.

"I don't know if I'm ready for that yet?" she said, embarrassed.

"Oh....ooohhh, damn baby, you never done it before?"

"No, I haven't, and I don't know if I'm ready just

yet. Are you mad?"

"*Mad?* Of course not, love. It's no pressure. We have all the time in the world for that. It'll happen when you're ready for it to happen."

Khloe felt comfortable when those words left Samir's mouth. She no longer felt pressured to lose her virginity, but hearing him say that she could take all the time she needed made her want to give in to him. She watched as he continued to get dressed. She decided that tonight after the party would be the night. She had just turned 14 years old, but she was ready to take that step into woman hood.

"Shay, I think I'm ready to have sex with Samir," she told her friend while she applied her make up.

"Oh my God... girl, really, that's a big step; are you really sure?"

"I am. I mean, he told me that I can take all the time I need, but I love him, and I want to make him happy."

"Khlo, listen to me... sex isn't going to make him happy. Samir isn't like all the rest of the street guys, and trust me, I know. He really loves you, and he'll wait for you. *You* make him happy, not your pussy."

"I know that, but I'm ready."

"Okay, well, it looks like your mind is made up. All I can tell you is relax, because it hurts, but the more you relax, the easier it will be."

"Well damn, you're making me want to change my mind," Khloe got nervous.

"I'm just saying, the first time won't be as pleasurable for either one of you, but it will get better."

Samir poked his head in to see if the ladies were ready and he couldn't stop gawking at how beautiful Khloe looked. He quickly snapped out of it and urged them to hurry up because it was already 12:30 and everyone was sitting around waiting on them.

When they finally emerged from the room, Meko couldn't help but notice Shay's ass filling out her dress.

"You are looking good as fuck," he whispered in her ear as they walked out the door.

"Is that right?" she teased as she rubbed her ass on his pelvis. She noticed him from the moment she walked in the door earlier that night. She knew she wanted him, but she had mastered the art of playing hard to get. Meko's fragrance filled her nostrils, and the sound of his voice in her ear made her wetter than Niagara Falls, but she knew she had to play it cool. She wasn't going to make it that easy for Meko Corleone. But she knew from the very moment he whispered in her ear that she was going to give it to him in the worst way possible.

Chapter Eleven

When the Corleones made it to the lobby of Samir's Building they saw five drivers holding signs with each of their names on them. Carlyle went all out for his son's Graduation; from throwing the biggest party, to making sure Samir and his Crew made a grand entrance in matching Rolls Royce's. They were more than hyped as they followed their drivers to their awaiting vehicles.

Samir watched with excitement as everyone loaded up. He knew tonight would be a night to remember, and for the first time in a long time, he relaxed. He could finally celebrate their accomplishments. He only wished his brothers could be there, but he could feel their presence all around him. He didn't have Sin and Ace, but he had Meko, Seven, Chase, and Cesar, and they were just as much his brothers as his blood brothers.

"Yo, Corleones, come over here for a second," he called them over to his car, "I just wanted y'all to know that tonight is about us, and what we about to

121

do to this game. I couldn't have asked for a better group of niggas to take this journey with, I love all y'all. We are Black Corleones for life, Joe," he told them as they each dapped each other.

They stood next to Samir's Rolls and posed for one last picture as a united front, because without knowing it, this night was about to change them as a crew and everything that they stood for as a family.

As they each departed to their respective vehicles, Meko grabbed Shay's hand and aggressively told her she was riding with him. She loved how he took control, so she followed him without any exception.

Once they were inside his car, he grabbed her and kissed her passionately. She could feel her pussy pulsating, but she immediately stopped him.

"Meko, as bad as I wanna fuck your brains out in this sexy ass car, I don't want to mess up my hair and makeup before the party," she told him.

"Fuck your hair and makeup. I'll take you tomorrow and buy you the makeup store and the salon too."

"As good as that sounds, you're gonna have to wait till after the party to taste this pussy, baby."

"Naw, I think I'll taste it now," he pulled her panties to the side and entered her vagina with his fingers. She was so wet her juices were trickling down his hand. She threw her head back in ecstasy as he increased his speed bringing her to the first orgasm she ever had from someone fingering her.

"Meko, stop, please!" she squealed as he invaded her insides, "Baby, please, I can't take it."

With a feeling of accomplishment, he did as he was asked, leaving her in a confused state. She made up in her mind in that very moment that Khloe wasn't the only one getting fucked that night. With the short encounter with Meko, her covenant, hard-to-get act went right out the window, along with her inhibitions.

When the Corleones arrived to the club, it was a madhouse outside. The line was wrapped around the building twice and the entire Chicago dope world was out in full effect. The parking lot and streets around the club looked like a luxury vehicle dealership, and everybody who was anybody came out to celebrate the Corleones graduation.

They each jumped out their cars with excitement as photographers snapped their pictures. The scene was something out of a music video. Everybody there was dressed to the nines, and when the Corleones finally made it inside the club, it was absolute insanity.

All the dope boys were in the building, young

and old. The feds would have had a field day if the stumbled across that party. The city's most beautiful women were in the building hoping to snag anyone of the ballers that attended that night. Security escorted the Corleones to their section.

When they got there, Casey and his crew were waiting. He had two duffle bags with over 500k in big bills as an early gift to his suppliers for their graduation. Carlyle made sure security escorted the money out of the club so there would be no discrepancies at the end of the night.

"Fucking with you is probably the best decision that we ever made, my nigga," Meko said to Casey as he hugged him.

"Shit, my net worth tripled since I been fucking with y'all. It's only right that I come lace my niggas right. I mean, it is a celebration," Casey laughed.

Once they settled into their sections, the champagne bottles came pouring in from all directions. Everybody was in a good mood, but when Samir looked around, Cesar was nowhere to be found. His crew was all together, but he was M.I.A; once again.

Seven tapped Samir on his shoulder and pointed to Cesar popping bottles with a well-known crew from 71st and Oglesby. They were one of the only crews that refused to cop from the Corleones and it forced them to make money with a crew from out west.

Samir watched in disbelief as Cesar laughed; popped bottles and out right kicked it with niggas that he knew had an issue with him, but he kept a level head and didn't let Cesar ruin his night. When Cesar returned to his section, he told Samir that the Oglesby Boys were sending over a couple of bottles of Dom P to congratulate them on all their success.

"What are you doing, Cesar?" Samir asked sternly.

"What you mean?"

"What the fuck are you doing with them niggas, bro?"

"Those are my people, and they some real solid niggas. I fuck with them cuz' they about they bread, and so are we, so what's the issue?"

"Don't even worry about it, bro." Samir said as he shook his head.

Just then Rocko, one of the Oglesby Boys came over to the Corleone section with bottles in hand. "Samir, congrats on your graduation; this is for you," he said as he handed him the bottle.

Samir didn't say a word to Rocko, he just looked at Cesar. He knew Rocko and his crew didn't really fuck with him like that, and he found it strange that Cesar would be associating himself with them.

"So, Sam, I wanted to talk business with you," Rocko continued, "I know you niggas getting money, but that ain't shit compared to what you could get if you fuck with us."

"No disrespect, but I'm not doing business right now. I'm here with my pops, my niggas and my girl. We celebrating, and right now ain't the time," Samir shut him down.

"Aight then, enjoy the rest of your night," he said, sarcastically as he walked away.

Samir wasn't about to let anything upset him. He had everything he wanted, and tonight was about enjoying the fruits of his labor.

What he didn't know, was that turning down Rocko's invitation would plant a seed even he wouldn't see growing.

Just as he was about to let his mind wonder, his father brought out his biggest surprise of the night. Samir was shocked when he saw *Jay-Z* walk into the V.I.P section to greet him. He was a huge *Jay-Z* fan, and his music was the soundtrack to his life. He couldn't believe his father made his dream of meeting him come true. This was one of the best nights of his life.

The crowd went nuts when *Jay-Z* took the microphone and wished Samir and his crew a happy graduation. It sent the Corleones into instant hood celebrity status amongst their peers. When it was all over, Carlyle succeeded in throwing the biggest graduation party Chicago had ever seen, and he managed to make his youngest son happy in the process.

On their way out the club, Samir noticed Cesar outside with Rocko and his crew. Cesar spent more time with them then he did with his own crew, and Samir was determined to find out what he had going on with them and why Rocko felt so comfortable approaching him. He knew Rocko had ill intentions toward him for a while now, and to see his right hand man kicking it with him left Samir with a bad taste in his mouth.

"Meko, have your young boy meet me at the condo tomorrow. I need to find out what Cesar got going on with these Oglesby Boys."

"No problem. I'm already on it, cuz' I didn't like that shit all night," Meko responded.

"Don't make Ces feel like we on to him, just find out what he got going on with them."

"That nigga foul right, SC? He know them niggas ain't never fucked with us from day one, and now he all in they face, kicking it in the club and shit," Seven chimed in as he walked up to his boys.

"That shit is shiesty to be honest with you," Chase also added his opinion.

"Yooo, Ces, we about to head to the pancake house!" Meko yelled across the parking lot.

"Aight bro, I'll catch up with you niggas later!"

"Naw nigga, we going as a crew, so let's roll!" Meko responded aggressively.

"I said I'm good, Mek!" Cesar bucked back as he jumped in Rocko's Lexus truck.

Meko didn't say another word because he knew Cesar was becoming a foul nigga. He was letting the money go to his head, but even Meko didn't believe Cesar was aligning himself with Rocko and his crew. For the first time in his life Meko didn't want to trust his gut feeling. Even he didn't think Cesar would go against the loyalty of their family.

Meanwhile, inside Rocko's truck, Cesar was painting a different picture of his loyalty to the Corleones. Cesar wanted to be the man, but he knew that would never happen as long as Samir was in the position of power. He knew linking up with Rocko would give him the position he desperately wanted.

"This nigga Meko ain't shit. You see how he try to talk to me, like I ain't second in command in this Corleone shit... nigga betta stand down before he get handled."

"Yea, he ain't got no respect, but why you *second* in command though, my guy? You're just as important to the crew as Samir. How come he gets to call all the shots, who that nigga think he is?"

"He think cuz' his pops put him on that make him the boss."

"But that nigga ain't even in the trenches, you putting in all the work, that nigga just sitting back collecting the money," Rocko said convincingly. He knew exactly what he was doing. He was planting a notion in an easily convinced Cesar so he could use Cesar to get to Samir. He never liked how quickly Samir and his crew came up in the game. His jealousy toward Samir and his success made him want to remove him completely out of the game, and he knew with Cesar's greed and ego, he would be an easy pawn in this chess match.

"That's exactly what I'm saying; this nigga Samir living life lavishly. Riding Rolls to graduation parties and flying niggas in. But yet, you say we all splitting this bread equally... nigga please. I ain't in a high rise condo down town," Cesar agreed.

But the fact of the matter was, Samir never under handed any of his boys and everybody that worked under his regime had a comfortable living. Cesar just was a loose cannon with money, and he blew his cash quicker than it came. While the rest of the Corleones were investing into legal endeavors to increase their net worth, Cesar was blowing 20 to 50k on bullshit, like taking hoes on trips, and turning up in strip clubs in Houston. He often had to borrow money from Samir, which left Samir vexed, because he was getting money just like the rest of them.

Cesar and Rocko spent most of the night talking about Samir, and Rocko soaked it all in as his mind began to devise a plan against the Corleones with Cesar at his inside.

Back on the south side of town, Samir and his crew made sure Casey made it to his hotel safe and headed back to his house. Everybody was beyond drunk, but the good thing was, his father made sure they had drivers to get them home safe.

Once the arrived at Samir's building, Seven and Chase headed home with their dates, and Meko decided to take Shay to his house so they could finish what they started.

"I'm not going with you," she teased.

"Why not?"

"Cuz', I have to stay with my friend."

"Go ahead girl. Meko will make sure you straight," Khloe encouraged her to go home with Meko, mainly because she thought that Meko would be a better man to her than those other clowns she normally dated. Besides, it would be perfect for her best friend to date her man's best friend.

Shay took Khloes advice and went with Meko; she wanted to go with him anyway. She hugged her friend and they left.

When they got to their apartment, Khloe hugged Samir from behind as he opened their door and softly whispered in his ear that she was ready to give him her virginity.

"Are you sure you're ready?"

"Yes, I'm sure. I just wanna make you happy."

"But I'm already happy. We don't need sex to make me happy, baby."

"I know, but I'm ready for you to make love to me, Samir," she told him as she grabbed his hand and led him to him their bedroom.

Once inside, Khloe made her move. She kissed him and unbuttoned his dress shirt. He gripped her breast as she came out of her clothes, never unlocking her lips from his. She moved toward their bed and lie down, pulling him on top of her. He kissed her all over as she felt her lower regions warm up from his hands caressing her.

He stopped, looked at her naked body and asked her once more was she sure she wanted this, she assured him that it was okay.

Samir was just as nervous as she was. Even though he had dealt with a few virgins; Khloe was different because he loved her.

He kissed her as he began to gently push himself inside of her tight pussy. She gasped and squeezed him as she tried to remember her friend's advice to relax.

"Are you okay? Do you want me to stop?" Samir asked, realizing he was hurting her.

"No, Samir, don't stop," she told him.

He continued to push himself inside of her. She screamed as she felt her cherry pop. He had every inch between her thighs. He stopped for only a moment to allow her to get familiar with the feeling of his dick inside her pussy, and then he began to stroke her slow and deep. The more he moved, the more she screamed, until her screams of pain turned into screams of pleasure.

"OOOOOHHHHH, Samir, I love you so much," she moaned as he fucked her.

"I love you too. Shit, this pussy is tight. You feel good as hell," he said as he increased his speed, sending shocks of ecstasy through her body.

"Samir, baby, oh God... I can't take it. I don't know what's going on," she said as she felt herself cumming for the first time.

He told her that she was about to nut and commanded that she let it out. He fucked her faster and faster as her pussy loosed up for him even more. The thought of her cumming excited him and brought him to his peak.

He gripped her ass as he felt himself about to nut. She screamed his name and right when he could feel her pussy spasm on his dick, he climaxed deep inside of her.

Breathing heavy and feeling drained, he kissed her slowly as the last bit of nut oozed out of his dick and into her pussy. He pulled out and they fell asleep in each other's arms.

The next morning Samir woke up with a slight hangover and Khloe asleep on his chest. He checked his two-way for any messages and started to think about the way Cesar was acting at their graduation party. He was starting to wonder what was going on in Cesar's mind, but he didn't want to assume the worse, so he texted him to meet up so they could talk about how he felt.

Samir didn't want to believe that Cesar was beginning to turn against them. He took his recent distance as Cesar just being Cesar, but he couldn't allow himself to believe that what was happening right under his nose was actually true.

He kissed Khloe on the forehead and got up to get dressed. He knew he had to get to the bottom of this Cesar issue before it came back to bite him the ass.

Phone ringing

"Yo, what's up?" Meko answered his phone, groggy.

"Mek, get up nigga. I need you to get on this Oglesby Boy shit with Cesar, right now," Samir said, sounding concerned.

"SC, come on bro, it's only....."

"Two thirty in the afternoon, my nigga. So, get out that pussy and get on it," he teased Meko.

"I ain't in no fucking pussy, Joe. I think I'm still drunk from last night. That shit was crazy. I don't even remember half of it."

"Well, do you remember Ces hopping in the whip with Rocko. You do remember Rocko, right?"

"Man, I'm still hot about that. What the fuck was this nigga thinking. Why is he even aligning himself with niggas who clearly don't fuck with us?"

"That's what I'm talking about. You can bring 'ol girl to my crib with Khloe, but I need you to put your ear to the streets and have lil' Carlos researching this shit for us."

"Aight G, I'm on it."

"And Meko, them niggas are Mickey Corbras, so hit up Valli and tell him to put the stones on alert, just as a precautionary measure."

"I got you."

Samir left a note and some money for Khloe and

headed out the door to meet Cesar. His mind was going to every scenario possible, but never once did it go to Cesar's impending betrayal.

He and Cesar grew up together; Cesar knew his weakness and his strengths. He brought Cesar in when everybody around him told him not to. He never thought he would see the day his very best friend was turning against him. His mind was wondering when his phone rang.

"Baby, where are you?" he heard Khloe ask when he picked up.

"I had to make a run babe. I left a note and some money for you to go shopping or something when Meko brings your girl over. I'll have a driver pick you up when you're ready."

"I wanted to have breakfast with you though."

"I'm sorry baby, but I promise, we can go to dinner tonight, anywhere you want."

"Well, okay then."

"Don't be like that Khlo, I had something very important to do."

"Okay, baby, it's cool. Someone is at the door anyway, so I'll see you tonight."

"Okay."

He could sense that she was upset about leaving her in the house, but she was going to have to understand that this was his life and sometimes there would be things she didn't like, and sometimes he would move in a way she wouldn't understand.

But Samir couldn't focus on Khloe at the moment; he had to focus on getting a handle on his crew before it proved to be detrimental.

Back at his house, Khloe was fuming because he left without even saying goodbye. She saw the money on the counter with a ten thousand dollar band around it and wondered to herself if this was what her life would be like. Her man always gone, but leaving stacks of money on the counter like it would make his absence any better.

She looked through her peephole and saw her best friend dressed in a brand new outfit that she didn't have on the night before.

"Ummm, bitch, where you get these clothes from, you didn't have a purse last night that was big enough to carry extra clothes?"

"Meko brought this for me, cuz' I was not about to be caught dead doing the walk of shame through your building in the same clothes I had on last night."

"Fucking for clothes, you ain't nothing but a hoe," Khloe teased.

"Bitch, whatever. So, how was your first time?"

"It would have been amazing if I didn't wake up

alone this afternoon."

"Khloe, don't you start with that nagging and tripping shit. You got a good ass nigga. Look how he got you living. He took you away from that hell hole of a life and he's giving you everything."

"Girl, I don't care about this stuff. I just want him. You like all this material stuff, and niggas leaving money on the counter like you're a hoe."

"Bitch, please... he left this money on the counter to make sure you were straight while he handled his business. It's time for you to stop playing a grown woman and start acting like one. Samir is a hustler baby... and he don't need to be dealing with his spoil brat girlfriend who wants him at home every second when he has to deal with the shit in the streets; be a good girl, Khloe... don't nag him."

Khloe didn't respond to Shay, but she did understand where she was coming from. She didn't want to cause Samir any unwanted strife when he was already dealing with so much being a young boss. She just wanted to be the kind of woman that he could come to and forget about his troubles and leave his worries at the door. Love wasn't even a strong enough word to describe how she felt about him. She felt bad for acting like a brat and knew she had to make it up to him, so that's exactly what she planned to do when he returned home.

In the meanwhile, she took the money he left her and took her friend out for a well needed girl's day in the Rolls Royce Samir had waiting for her.

Samir, on the other hand wasn't having the same good day as Shay and Khloe. Feeling like he didn't have a handle on his own operation was starting to get under his skin more than he would have liked to admit. But he wasn't going to assume the worst before he spoke to Cesar.

When he pulled up to Pepe's restaurant on 147th in the burbs, he saw Cesar's car parked. He pulled into the small parking lot and collected his thoughts before he went inside. Once in the restaurant, he spotted his boy and joined him at the table.

"SC, what's up with you? Last night was crazy," Cesar laughed as he hugged Samir.

"Yea, it was, but that's exactly what I wanna talk to you about. Ces, bro, we been down since we been in diapers. Are you not happy with this family?" Samir got straight to the point.

"What kinda fucking question is that for you to be asking me? I help start this family. I'm just as much a Black Corleone as any one of you niggas," Cesar retaliated.

"I never said you weren't, but Black Corleones' ride for each other, and with each other. Just keep it real, why you kicking with Rocko and the Oglesby Boys?"

"First off, Samir, don't come questioning me about shit I do, cuz' I'm a grown ass man. I was kicking with Rocko cuz' that's my nigga. Shit, it was graduation night and my niggas came out to celebrate with me."

"Those are your niggas, right? The Oglesby Boys are *your* niggas, huh? What about the Black Corleones, are we *your* niggas? Cuz' you damn sure ain't been acting like it. Since when did a group of niggas who never wanted to see us shine become *your* niggas? Since when did a group of niggas who the whole city knows don't fuck with the Black Corleones, become buddy, buddy with a Black Corleone, Cesar? Please inform me on the matter, cuz' I need to know where I been all this time while my second in command been linking up with my rival."

"Your rival, SC? See, I'm starting to feel like this shit has become all about *Samir Kendal aka Samir Corleone.* It's always *your* crew and *your* operation. Everything is about you, Sam... and you too blind to see it. Ever since that nigga Kyle fucked up, you've been different. How you call me second in command, the capo, but yet you call Meko for everything. Am, I really second in command, Sam, or is that just something you talking cuz' you salty behind Rocko and the Oglesby Boys. When we started this shit it was about us, The Black Fucking Corleones. Now, all I hear is Samir and the Corleones, like we ain't put in as much work as you."

"So, that's what this is about, huh?" You want people to say your name. You wanna be the man, huh? Let me make one thing clear Ces, I don't give a fuck about what the streets got to say about what goes on inside this crew, because we know what the real is. Niggas gon' keep talking, but we keep making the profit they can't. And you my nigga, doing what you did last night in front of everybody gives them something to talk about, and you know what they saying. They saying the Black Corleone foundation is weak. They saying that we can't even hold on to our core as a crew, so how could we possibly hold on to our operation, and you fucking with niggas who's known not to fuck with us just gives them ammo. Yet, you're so blinded by the fucking titles that you can't even see what you doing to us on the back end."

On some levels, Cesar knew everything Samir was saying was right, but he couldn't see past his ego. Being a Corleone changed his life, but he didn't see it that way. He didn't feel respected and the

Oglesby Boys where feeding his undeserving ego by making him think he was above the other members of the Black Corleone family.

They manipulated his pride and greed by making him feel like they had his back more than his own crew. Cesar could feel his loyalty shifting, but he wasn't ready to walk away from being a Black Corleone because he helped build this empire and he and Samir were friends their whole lives.

He knew he could always smooth things over with Samir, but it was time he started setting himself up to be in control of his own shit, without the Corleones.

He decided to ease the situation with Samir and make him feel comfortable. He apologized on how shit looked at the party and assured Samir that those where not his intentions.

"I'm down with this family, SC, been down since day one. This is my fam, we Black Corleones till the casket drop."

"I just need to know one thing Cesar?"

"What's that, Joe?"

"You making side deals with these Oglesby Boys or not?"

Cesar looked Samir straight in his eyes and didn't speak for what felt like an eternity. "Naw, Samir... I would never make a deal with anybody without going to a vote," he lied.

In fact, he had already started supplying the Oglesby Boys without the other Corleones knowledge. His greed was about to put a big dent in the Corleone universe, and Samir and the rest of the Corleones would never see it coming.

Chapter Twelve

The time flew by and each New Year brought on new possibilities as the Corleones began to settle into their life as full time dope boys. Their expansion down south had more than quadrupled in profit and the demand had forced them into Mississippi, Alabama and they were in talks with a crew out of Atlanta that was getting big money. They sought out the young Corleones during a short visit to Chicago.

The Corleones, now in their early twenties began to look at life beyond just selling dope. They set a precedent in the game at an age most would have deemed impossible, but they knew this life wouldn't last them forever, and the dynamics of their once tight knit crew had begun to drastically change.

Cesar was turning into someone none of them knew. His intense need to be the man was causing a rift in their family that somehow went unnoticed by Samir.

After their high school graduation, Samir kept a tight watch on Cesar's movements, but nothing ever panned out to raise a red flag in his mind. Cesar knew after that he had to play the part of being loyal to a family he felt didn't respect him or his position. But once the heat was off him, he went back to his jealous ways.

He continued to do business with the Oglesby Boys and even started supplying them without Samir and the rest of the crew's knowledge. He made sure Valli didn't get suspicious by making it look like his sets where moving more work than usual. But the one thing Cesar couldn't avoid was the talk on the street. He knew eventually word would get out about his dealings with Rocko and his crew, but he didn't care, because Rocko manipulated him into believing he was running the Oglesby Boy crew.

His plan was to use Cesar as much as he could and eventually take over the streets using the work he supplied him with.

While the rest of the Corleones were investing in legal endeavors, Cesar was blowing more money than he was actually pulling in. He managed to make sure he paid what his sets owed, but his

Rockefeller lifestyle was catching up to him.

The Corleones met at Samir's condo once a week for poker night, and to discuss the nature of their business, but Cesar was M.I.A. so much, it came to the point where the others were beginning to pressure Samir about voting him out.

"Cesar been with us since we started this thing four years ago," twenty one year old Samir interjected.

"Man, SC, fuck that. This nigga is never around, and he ain't been handling business at all. I hear he still fucking with them Oglesby niggas too, and I don't like that shit," Seven responded.

"I've been hearing the same thing around my sets," Chase added.

"I've been telling you niggas I don't trust him. Since were sixteen, seventeen years old. Ever since we expanded, that nigga been real big headed and shit, running round here with his head up his ass, blowing cash like water; this nigga making the same money we making, but yet, he living in a fucking apartment. Come on Sam, something just ain't adding up," Meko spoke his peace.

"I'm saying; we need to handle this situation before it ends up handling us. Because this nigga Ces hasn't been acting like a Corleone lately, and we all see it but you, SC," Seven told Samir.

"What, y'all don't think I hear the same shit y'all hear? I'm in the same streets y'all in. I'm running the same operation y'all running. But Cesar is a part of this family, and we have a loyalty to this family no matter what. Niggas been trying to take our spot since the second we got in this game, and if we dismantle Cesar's position, how y'all think that's gon' look?" Samir replied.

"It's gon' look like we got rid of the snake in the grass before it bit us in the ass," Meko said.

Later that night Samir went to bed with his mind racing. He knew Meko, Seven and Chase were right about Cesar, but his loyalty was getting the best of him. This was not the time for them to fall apart because they had too much riding on their possible expansion with the crew out of Atlanta.

He lay in his bed, staring at the ceiling in silence. Khloe could sense something was wrong, but she tried not to ask him about his business because she felt that wasn't her place. She just wanted to make sure he didn't stress too much. He had taught her so much about life in the few short years they were together. He didn't shield her from his life, but he didn't involve her with everything either. He taught her the aspects of the game he had to learn on his own, and some he learned from his brothers and his father. He made sure she would be able to hold her own if anything was to happen to him.

She respected him on a level she never respected anyone in her life. He taught her what it was to be a woman, and what it meant to carve out your own way in life. Her only wish was to take away his stress. She saw him age so much over the last year from his business becoming more strenuous and intense. Through it all, she made sure that his home life was easy, but she knew something more than the woes of the game was getting to him.

"I took Kelsey and his brother the money today, babe," she said softly as she climbed on top of him.

"Okay babe, thank you."

"My guidance counselor at school said I should have enough credits to graduate this year if I wanted to."

"Oh yeah, that's good baby, I'm proud of you."

"Yea, you should be, you pushed the shit out of me about school."

"Well, I wanted to make sure you know how important it is for a woman to be educated. A pretty face is nice, but a woman with a brain is unstoppable."

"What's wrong baby. Why are you so stressed?" she asked him hoping he would let her in.

"Nothing Khlo, I'm good. I got things handled okay, don't worry about me."

147

"How can I not worry when you're involved in such a dangerous lifestyle?"

"Listen, just kiss me."

She didn't press the issue; she just did what he asked. He didn't let her in on the situation with Cesar. He made love to her four times that night, each time coming inside her, hoping to create another part of himself.

Being inside her loins was the only time his mind was clear. Being with her made him forget about all the bullshit he was going through in the streets.

The next morning he woke up to the non-stop ringing of his phone.

"You have a collect phone call from an inmate in the Cook County Jail, would you like to accept the charges?" the operated asked.

"Yea, I'll accept."

"Samir, what's up with you?" Sin's voice sounded weary on the phone. Being in jail for the last 4 years was taking a toll on him.

"I'm good bro, how are you?"

"We cool little bro, glad this little bid is coming to an end. But this ain't a social call. You need to come down here and see us, we need to talk."

"Look, Sin, don't worry about it, I got it handled."

"I'm sure you do, but bring your ass down here tomorrow, you hear me?"

"Yea bro, I hear you. I'll be there."

Samir knew exactly what Sin and Ace wanted to talk to him about. He knew he had to get a handle on this Cesar thing, and voting him out the crew was starting to look more like his only option. It was one thing to have Meko, Seven and Chase encouraging the decision, but to have his brothers looking at him like he couldn't handle himself wasn't an image he was comfortable living with.

Samir knew he couldn't go back to sleep, so he got up and headed to check on Valli. Valli informed him that Cesar was doing his re-ups more often than usual, and at first Valli didn't look at it like a problem, but he was requesting more work than he was supposed to get.

Valli told Cesar he had to talk to Samir before releasing the work and Cesar lost his cool. Valli held his ground, but Cesar was highly upset.

"Nigga was talking mad reckless, talking about he run this Corleone shit and he didn't need no permission from you to do what he needed to do."

"Have you heard of his sets pushing more work than usual?"

"Naw, I fuck with a few niggas in that area and they ain't told me they moving more work than normal. I don't know where this increase came from," Valli informed Samir.

"Okay, well let me handle Cesar. Is it making us short anywhere else?"

"Naw, we good right now,"

"Give him what he came for, but keep a tail on him and find out where the work is going. If it's not going to his sets, I'ma put my young boy back on it. If anything comes up that you feel is amiss, let me know."

"Okay, I got you SC. Don't even trip. If it's some bogus shit going on, I'll find it," Valli assured him.

Samir wasn't feeling good about what was going on under his nose. He couldn't bring himself to believe Cesar was biting the hands that fed him. He began to question himself and his loyalty to Cesar.

He had a meeting with his father about a new venture and a new connect, so he had to put Cesar to the back of his mind and hold his composure in front of his father and Carlyle's counterparts.

He drove in silence thinking about how much things changed since he was that 16 year old boy trying to jump in the game and build an empire with his best friends. He never knew that the more money they bought in would begin to change the promise they made to each other four years earlier. Deep down, Samir knew Cesar changed, but he didn't want to believe it.

When he pulled in front of the restaurant where his father was, his palms were sweaty and his stomach was in knots. He knew if his brothers knew about Cesar; his father knew first.

When Samir walked inside he was lead to his father's table. He noticed an older Spanish guy that he never seen before sitting with him. He sat down next to Carlyle, confused as to what this meeting was about.

"Son, this is Paoulo, Paoulo, this is my son, Samir. The one I was telling you about," Carlyle introduced them.

"Nice to meet you,"

"Same here, I've heard a lot about you and your black Corleone crew."

"I called you here today, Samir because Paoulo needs a good crew to set him up in the Chicago market, and right now the Co-op can't handle what he needs, so I think it's time you graduate from having a middle man and go straight to your own source."

"What? Pops, what exactly are you saying?" he asked in shock.

"What I'm saying is, you and Paoulo here should build a nice little business relationship, and instead of your old man being your connect, it's time you have your very own connect."

"What your father here is trying to tell you son, is I need a crew with heart and loyalty to distribute my product, and with everything you got going, I think you are the man for the Job. Can you handle two hundred kilos a month, at forty five hundred a key?"

"Yes sir, Mr. Paoulo, I can handle it," Samir responded, still in shock about this opportunity.

"Well, good then, it's settled. Let's shake on it. I will contact your old man with a time to meet your entire crew very soon," Paoulo informed Samir.

"I know about Cesar and those Oglesby Boys, Sam. Get a handle on that shit now, because this is a huge opportunity to finally be your own man, but one bad apple can fuck it all up," Carlyle warned Samir as he walked him to the car.

"Dad, I got it handled," Samir assured him.

He hit Meko and made sure to have the crew meet him in the gardens to let them know about his meeting. He knew with this new opportunity coming their way, their empire was about to explode. He was honored his father trusted him with this chance at having his own connect and the ability to run shit his way for the first time in his career.

They would really be able to flood the streets,

especially his expansion.

When he made it to the gardens, Meko, Seven and Chase where already standing outside the trap, talking to Valli. Once again, Cesar was M.I.A.

"Mek, you didn't hit Cesar?" he asked as he greeted his crew.

"Yea, I did, but he didn't answer me back."

"Okay, we don't have time to wait for that nigga. Valli, you got on that right?"

"Yea boss, I got it under control."

"Okay, good. Fellas, I just left a meeting with my pops and shit is about to get really real. He introduced me to a Spanish nigga named Paoulo and the Corloenes have officially shook hands with our own connect," he told his crew in excitement.

"Stop playing, Joe," Seven joked.

"I'm not playing. This nigga is about to hit us with two hundred keys a month at forty five hundred a key."

"Oh shit. So, what you saying is, we can cop what we want when we want. No re-up rules?" Meko inquired.

"That's exactly what I'm saying. But we gon' do things a little different though. We gon' keep copping from my pops and keep our sets booming with that, and just hit our expansion with what we get from Paoulo. Only niggas moving major weight get this work outside of our expansions, and I'm gon' take that meeting with them Atlanta boys and work a deal with them. This is the big time fellas."

"Are we ready for this, SC?" Chase asked.

"My pops feels we are, so I say we are," he responded. "I'm going to consult my brothers tomorrow about this and that...."

Just as he was finishing his statement Cesar pulled up. He wasn't too enthused about being there, but he had to keep up appearances, plus Valli called him about his re-up just as Samir had asked him to.

Cesar spoke to his crew and went inside to handle his business with Valli. After 20 minutes, he emerged from the house carrying the duffle bag containing the work that was supposed to be going to his sets, but instead, it was being supplied to the Oglesby boys.

"What's up family, what we meeting about?" he casually asked.

"Had you been here when the rest of us got here you would've known," Meko barked.

"Mek what's the deal with you? I'm here now aren't I?" he tried to keep the peace.

"Yea Joe, you here now," Meko decided not to let himself get upset behind Cesar. He knew eventually he would slip up, and he would be right there waiting for him.

"We were meeting about our new connect my pops just linked us with," Samir interrupted.

"New connect, what you mean new connect?"

"My pops linked me with a Spanish nigga named Paoulo. My pops can't take on another connect cuz' he dealing with the Colombians, so he passed it along to me."

"What this Spanish papi talking about?"

"He's talking at least two hundred a month at forty five hundred a unit."

"Damn, those are big numbers, how we gon' move that kinda of work?"

"You really should have been here when SC called the meeting, Joe. This shit is annoying," Seven Chimed in, "As a matter of fact, what's so important that you ain't never around, aren't you apart of this family?"

"I been a part of this family from day one, so don't ever question my involvement in some shit I helped start. I don't need to be around you niggas twenty four seven. I mean damn, I do have sets to fucking run," Cesar snapped.

"Well, if you were running your shit effectively that shit would practically run itself. My shit run so smooth I only got go around on collect day," Chase added in his calm demeanor.

155

"Good for you nigga," Cesar snapped at him.

"Look, now ain't the time for this shit. We don't need to be falling apart right now, not with this fucking shit in our laps. This shit is about to make us multimillionaires, and I really don't wanna hear this shit. We sound like females. We'll deal with this later."

"I ain't the one with the problem, these niggas always starting shit," Cesar told him.

"I don't care, Joe, damn. To answer your question, we're gonna use the new work to supply our expansions and keep copping from my pops to supply our home front. I'm going to Atlanta to fuck with some niggas out there, so that's another avenue. Our niggas in Virginia move big numbers, so we'll supply them with this shit, and only niggas copping major units. Next Week we're going to Gurney to meet with Paoulo as unit, everybody needs to be there. Now, if you niggas don't mind, I promised Ms. Khloe a dinner date, so I'm going home," Samir told them as he ended their meeting.

"SC, ask Khlo if she going with Kaiyah tomorrow to pick out salons," Seven asked.

"Why is Kai still running around, ain't y'all about to have a baby any second now?" Samir asked as he got in his car."

"Yea, but you know she hard headed as hell. I

promised her when she graduated I would buy her a salon; she won't let that shit go."

"You niggas are whipped," Meko laughed from his car window

"Sprung as fuck!" Chase chimed in.

"Yeah, okay, I'm whipped alright. That's why you two niggas together, looking for pussy when I already got it at home, waiting for me," Samir joked.

On the outside looking in The Corleones seemed to be living the life. Their reign in the drug game was only getting better. It seemed as if they had it all. Investments, hood fame, love and money, but their foundation was cracking right under them and they couldn't feel it.

As they continued to move in their success, Cesar's greed was getting the best of him. His insatiable appetite for being the man was only growing bigger. Seven, Meko, Chase and Samir didn't realize that this new opportunity would be more of a curse than a blessing.

Chapter Thirteen

"You nervous bro?" Chase asked Seven as they awaited the arrival of the first born Black Corleone baby.

"Naw, I'm not nervous, I'm just anxious to finally meet my little man."

"I can't believe one of us is about to have a baby. I can't lie to you fam, I'd be nervous as shit right now. Fatherhood is a big step," Samir chimed in.

"Yea, but I'm excited about it. I didn't have a father around, so I'm glad that I got a son to be the kind of father he wasn't. I envied the relationship you and your pops got, SC, cuz' I always wanted that shit."

"Look at it this way Sev, at least you got a chance to change that never ending cycle of little niggas coming up without a pops," Meko added.

The impending birth of Seven's son brought out a softer side of the otherwise serious business savvy

Corleones. They never thought their lives would change so much the day got together at Meko's grandmother's house to devise their takeover in Chicago's drug world. Now, one of them was about to become a father.

They did everything as a unit, so it was no surprise that they would be together at the hospital awaiting the arrival of Seven's son. But there was one person who was absent to the occasion, and it happened to be Cesar.

It had gotten to a point where the other Corleones stop expecting Cesar to be around for their milestones, and he was rarely around for their business matters.

It had been two weeks since their last meeting in the gardens and Cesar was missing in action ever since. Samir was still waiting on word from Valli, but he made sure to put Meko's soldier Carlos on the job.

He was determined to find out what Cesar was up to. He tried not to think about the game with his Godson about to be born at any moment, but the fact was, they never truly got away from who they had become.

"What happened when you went to see Sin and Ace, Joe?" Meko asked as they headed to the hospital cafeteria.

"They got on my ass about this Cesar shit," Samir replied.

"Oh word. What did they say?"

"You know Sincere. He was just like, the shit didn't look good, especially in front of everybody, and basically, why am I'm pretending like I don't see what's happening right under my nose."

"Did you tell them about the extra work he copping?"

"Hell naw, Joe, that shit would have made things worst. My brothers are already on edge about missing out on showing me the ropes, and plus they feel like they gotta protect me, and they cant."

"Did they tell you how to move about this situation?"

"Ace said don't make no sudden moves until I know for sure what's going on. He said if Ces is on some snake shit or some underhand type shit, then moving to soon would fuck me up in the end. But again, you know Sin was on some snuff him type shit."

"How you wanna proceed?"

"I'm gon' take Ace's route and find out for a fact before we make any sudden moves."

"And if he is under handing us?"

"I don't know how I'll react, Mek, to be real with you. That nigga is like my brother."

"He's my brother too, Samir, but this is business, it's nothing personal, and we can't have a snake in our ranks, bro, we just can't," Meko implored.

Just as Samir was about to respond, Seven chirped them and told them that Kaiyah was about to give birth any second.

Meko and Samir dropped what they were doing and ran back up to the labor and delivery unit. Just as they approached Kaiyah's room they heard the first cries of the new baby Black Corleone, and the three of them became emotional.

Although Seven was the only one allowed in the room at the time, they made an exception and let his crew in to see his son.

Looking at the little boy Seven named Carson Chase Simmons, they all became emotional. They had been through it all since their middle school days. From fist fights, to their first girlfriends, to joining the game, and now witnessing the birth of one of their children; it solidified the Black Corleones as more than a street crew; they were just as much family as any blood family could be.

Right then they could feel their bond getting stronger as they each promised to always be there for Carson. Carson was lucky because he didn't gain one father, he gained four. Meko, Chase and Samir made a vow to Seven that no matter what happened in their lives, Carson would always be taken care of.

Seven understood the loyalty his crew had for him, but his joy would be short lived when Valli and Carlos sent each of them an urgent message.

"Man, this shit can wait?" Samir said as got his chance to hold baby Carson for the first time.

"The message is about Cesar, SC." Seven told him.

"Meko, go find out what the deal is," Samir ordered.

"I'm on it bro."

"Damn, I can't believe you got a kid, Seven," Chase said.

"Shit, me either."

"You know that means Sev fuck with me the toughest, cuz' he got my name as his middle name," Chase Joked.

"Nigga, fuck you, he only chose Chase as a middle name cuz' he on some white boy shit. I mean, the little nigga name is Carson for Pete's sake."

"Don't call this baby a nigga, Samir," Khloe quickly scolded him as she attended to Kaiyah.

"I'm sorry, baby," Samir joked as he kissed her forehead.

"I know, you're next, Samir." Kaiyah said as she held her son for the first time.

"Ummmm... girl, no we're not having no baby anytime soon. I'm trying to graduate this summer, and I don't see no ring on this finger," Khloe jumped in.

"You don't see a ring yet," Samir corrected.

In fact, he was thinking of proposing to Khloe for quite some time now. They been together a few years and he walked around with a ring he brought in his pocket every day, just trying to work up the nerve to ask her.

He didn't want to take away from Seven's moment, but he felt like this was just as good a moment as any. But just as he was about to get the courage to ask her, Meko walked in informing them that he needed them in the hallway ASAP.

"What's up Meko? I was just about to do something important," Samir said.

"I found out what's been going on with Cesar."

"Come on nigga, stop stalling. This Cesar bullshit interrupted the best day of my life... speak, my nigga," Seven snapped.

"What's up Mek, just tell us," Samir was afraid to hear the answer.

"Turns out Cesar been supplying the Oglesby Boys with our work and keeping the money for himself. The extra work he takes on his re-up hasn't been going to his sets, it's been going to them niggas, but he's not giving Valli the extra bread off top. Valli didn't say anything at first because it was Cesar, and he thought it was something we were all aware of, but once Valli told him he had to talk to you before he gave him more than normal, Cesar's reaction put him on alert," Meko told them.

"Are you sure?" Samir asked.

"Come on SC, damn, we had niggas get on the job and this is what they found out. I know you don't wanna believe it, but Cesar been real funny lately, my nigga, and you can't deny that shit," Meko barked.

"How you want us to handle this shit, Samir?" Seven asked.

"I don't want us to handle anything. I'll handle this myself," Samir replied.

"No disrespect, SC, but we're a family and Cesar is fucking us as a family, so this ain't something you gon' handle on your own," Chase spoke up.

"Chase, seriously, let me deal with Cesar."

"Sorry, but we're putting this to a vote. That's how we do shit around here. This isn't about you and Cesar, it's about us. So, all in favor of us handling this shit together, vote now," Chase commanded.

"I vote yay," Meko went first.

"Yay," Seven voted.

"I vote hell yes!" Chase added. "That's three to one, SC. We'll be handling this Cesar shit as a unit."

Samir knew he couldn't interject because this is the way they've always made their decisions. He had to respect the fact that he was out voted, but this was more of a personal issue, rather than a family one. Cesar was his friend the longest, so Samir knew deep down this wasn't a stab at the crew, this was jab at him. But he knew Meko, Seven, and Chase's loyalty to him would never allow them to see it that way. They always had his back, and this would be no different.

Reality began to set in that Cesar was really turning against him, and he was more hurt than angry.

"What you want us to do about these Oglesby niggas?" Meko asked.

"Let's hold off on them niggas, cuz' right now they think it's sweet, they getting my work and ain't paying for it; so what we gon' do is cut the head off the beast and the rest of the body will fall."

"You wanna deal with Cesar?" Seven interjected.

"Exactly!"

"How you wanna go about it?" Chase asked.

"We gon' make Ces think we hit a drought; cut his sets completely off. Let Valli know that nothing is to go out to Cesar or none of the sets he's running. And when he come around, Valli is to tell him my pops cut us off because the boys are snooping again. It's a precautionary measure. Eventually the nigga is gonna be in a pressure cooker situation, because them Oglesby Boys are snake niggas, and they gon' wanna keep the deal they got going with Cesar, and when he can't deliver, he gon' have to come to us. Meko, you and Chase head to Atlanta to fuck with them boys and when y'all get back we gotta make a Houston run because they need a re-up and we're gonna personally deliver it, but I'm gon' have Khloe take it. Cesar gon' be a part of that Houston trip and it'll be his last trip as a Black Corleone, because when we get back we're going to dismantle that crew and send Cesar a little message."

"Not for nothing, Joe, but I knew from day one that nigga Cesar was a snake, and now he just proved that his love ain't loyal," Meko added.

Chapter Fourteen

A few months passed and the Corleones set their plan into action to out Cesar. They started by cutting off supply to his sets, but making sure the people affected were taking care of through the rest of their operation. Samir put all Cesar's workers on alert, and even commissioned Cesar's top clientele on what he felt he had to do.

A lot changed since the Corleones found out about Cesar's disloyalty to their family. They began moving major work for Paoulo, but managed to keep their plan going of cutting Cesar out, despite all the work they were moving. They tried to operate as normal as possible without tipping him off to their plan.

Seven finally moved Kaiyah into her Salon and Khloe celebrated graduating from high school a year early; Samir couldn't have been more proud. Even though they were moving their operation into legal endeavors, their trap game flourished as Meko and Chase finally took the trip to Atlanta to see how things could work in expanding into the Georgia turf. After seeing the Atlanta boys in their element, Meko wasn't confidant that linking with them and his crew wouldn't be beneficial to their operation.

"But what happened, Mek?" Samir asked as they drove to check on Valli, and to collect the money for the month.

"Niggas is just way too out in the open, living life like it's a rap video," Meko replied.

"So, what are you saying?"

"I'm saying, I got a good feeling that their shit is about to come to an end, real quick, and I don't want us to be caught up in that shit when the feds come knocking."

"You didn't make him feel that you didn't wanna fuck with him, did you?"

"Naw, I keep shit sweet. Just let the nigga know how we operate and that I would have to get with the team and get back with him."

"Okay, good, so how you think we should move forward?"

"We don't, that's what I'm saying to you. I don't feel like it's a good look for us because that house of cards is about to come crashing down. I feel it in my gut."

"Cool, then it's a wrap. Mek, I need to say this to you. I should have trusted in your instinct from the very beginning. You always had my back and never steered me wrong. You should have been my right hand since day one, but its better late than never, right?"

"Don't even sweat that shit, SC. You're my brother and I don't give a fuck about titles. I chose to hold you down because you've always held me down. Without you, I wouldn't even be here; we gon' rock till the casket drop, my nigga."

Samir knew he could trust Meko with his life, so making him second in command was a logical choice.

While Samir and Meko's bond grew stronger, Cesar was stressing. He had been cut off by Samir without his knowledge and the pressure from the Oglesby Boys to keep supplying them was driving him to desperation. He paid Valli a visit almost every day since the decision to fake a drought had been set into action. Cesar knew he was losing his grip on his part of the Black Corleone operation, and he only had himself to blame. Rocko wasn't letting up because he didn't believe that a crew who was moving metro tons was all of a sudden in a drought when the rest of the city was doing fine.

"I just don't trust that shit, Cesar. It's something

fishy going on over there," Rocko explained.

"My niggas say we hit a drought. What the fuck you want me to do about that?" Cesar said desperately.

"But didn't you say y'all just linked up with y'all own connect for more than two hundred birds a month, and how confidant are you that those niggas are really *your* niggas? I heard in the hood that these niggas are living lavishly. My people say Samir's girl walk around in mink coats every day, and he just copped her a Escalade for her graduation, and a four hundred thousand dollar crib in Dynasty Lakes. How a nigga going through a drought spending money on his girl like water? Them niggas are cutting you out of the shit you built, my G," Rocko continued to play Cesar like a puppet.

"You're right, Roc, niggas have been eating mighty good, and this nigga Seven just bought his lady a state of the art salon and shit. I can't take these niggas playing me. I been knowing the money was equal from the beginning, but Samir conniving ass insisted the books where straight," Cesar fell right into Rocko's hand."

"What you gon' do about that?"

"We supposed to be taking a trip to Houston soon, and when we get back I'll let you know what we gon' do about this little situation."

On the other side of town Samir was handling business as usual when Valli informed him and Meko that Cesar was getting real antsy about the fake drought.

"Nigga calls me like forty times a day, Joe," Valli told them.

"Don't worry about him. Just keep doing what you doing and make sure Lil' Los keeps a handle on everything in Cesar's sets."

"What's y'all plan though, cuz' that nigga need to be erased."

"Don't concern yourself with family business, Valli. Just do your part in this, Joe. We'll take care of the rest," Meko ordered.

Samir was feeling uneasy about the situation. It hurt him to his core to handle his very best friend this way, but it hurt him even more to know that it was Cesar who turned.

He couldn't believe Cesar would bite their hand when all he had to do was come to him and Samir would have given him anything. Cesar's greed and determination to be top dog was destroying everything Samir wanted to build. It was never about money to him, it was always about family. Samir didn't realize it at the time, but things were only about to get worse with Cesar, because as much as he tried to shield Khloe from the hardships of the game as he groomed her, she was learning more than he wanted her too.

That night when he returned home, he could sense she wasn't too happy. The look on her face was one he had only seen one other time since they had been together. For a moment they sat in silence as she made him dinner, but it was starting to drive Samir crazy.

"Khloe, do you love me?" he asked, breaking their silence.

"Do you even have to ask, Samir?"

"I mean, like, do you love me to the point that you would do anything for me, no questions asked?"

"Yes, Samir, I love you. But why are you asking me this?"

"Because I need to take a trip to Houston soon,"

"Okay, but why are you telling me?"

"Because, this ain't no ordinary trip. I need to make a run and I need you to drive."

"So, I'll go with you and drive."

"Naw, baby, I need you and Shay to make the run. I'm not going to drive with you. I'm going to meet you there."

"Wait, what do you mean when you say run?"

"I need you to drive the work to Houston,

because four niggas in a whip with out of town plates is red flag on the interstate, so I need you to do this, Khloe."

"When?"

"Thursday,"

"But that's the day after tomorrow Samir?"

"I know, but I'm on a time crunch."

"Whatever you say, but before I do this, I have to tell you something."

"What's up?"

"Well, today Shay and I was in the city and I saw one of my friends from school and he told me to tell you that you need to watch your back. What's going on with Cesar, cuz' he said that Cesar is betraying you."

"Khloe, stop listening to everything somebody has to say."

"What do you mean stop listening to people. He said that Cesar is crossing you. I never liked his ass anyway. I always felt like he was jealous of you, and now you tryna tell me not to listen to people. People telling me that something could happen to you."

"Khloe, I said stop fucking listening to what the fuck people have to say. Niggas don't know what they talking about. You don't think I know what the fuck I'm doing out here. I been running my shit way before you came along. I don't need you or nobody else telling me about shit. I can handle my fucking self," Samir argued.

It was the first time he had ever raised his voice at her, and her reaction immediately made him regret it. It wasn't his intentions to take his frustrations out on her, but having her bring it up made it feel more close to home. He was finally realizing the severity of the situation.

Khloe didn't say a word as her eyes filled with tears. She ran off into their bedroom and slammed the door. She couldn't believe he had talked to her in such a matter. It broke her heart.

She knew he was stressed, but he never let it affect the way he treated her. Samir felt horrible about the way he spoke to her. He never wanted to make her feel pain, he had treated her like a queen all these years. Being Samir Corleone was starting to take a toll on him, but she was his peace in the midst of his chaotic lifestyle. He could hear her crying in the other room and it crushed his heart.

"Khloe, can I come in?" he asked as he knocked on their bedroom door.

"It doesn't matter, do what you want, this is your house, isn't it?"

"Listen, baby, I'm really sorry for yelling at you. It's just that this life is hectic and I hear enough of this bullshit in the streets, so when I come home to you, I don't wanna think about it. I'm sorry; please don't be made at me."

"Samir, you promised that you would never hurt me," she cried.

"I know baby, I didn't mean to hurt you," he said, as he kneeled down in front of her.

"I feel like shit, Khlo. I need you in my life, you're my world and I never wanna see you cry. I love you and I'm sorry," he told her, kissing her. She wanted to stop him, but she knew his words were genuine, so she allowed him to lay her down as he kissed her gently. She closed her eyes as he removed her shorts and began to kiss her pussy as if he was tongue kissing her actual lips.

Khloe tossed her head back in ecstasy as she felt her nut mounting. She grabbed his head and let out a loud scream while cumming hard on his tongue.

"Oooooh, my God; Samir, I love you baby!" she screamed as he increased the speed of his tongue, causing her to cum three more times before he eased his dick deep inside her. He made love to her slowly as he felt her vaginal muscles contracting on his dick.

"Khloe, I love you, have my baby, please," he whispered, driving his dick deep inside of her, trying to feel every inch of her pussy.

She gripped him tighter with every stroke. She loved him more and more every day and couldn't imagine her life without him. She could feel herself cumming with ever thrust of his hips, until she begged him to cum inside of her because her body couldn't take it anymore. Her request turned him on; to the point he increased his speed. The faster he went, the harder she came. The wetness of her vagina made him lose control, until he reached his peak and came harder than he ever came in his life.

That night they lie in each other's arms. They had no idea their lives were about to change forever.

Thursday rolled around and Khloe was nervous about being so involved with Samir's operation. She wanted to please him, but she didn't know if she had the guts to go through with an 18 hour drive to Texas with a truck full of cocaine.

Shay had always had Khloe's back, and she even thought this trip was too much for Khloe to take on, but she wasn't going to let her go alone, so she went along with her, because that's what friends do. Samir could've put anybody on the job, but he wanted Khloe to learn every aspect of the game.

"You sure you want her to do this, Joe. I mean, what if she gets pulled over?" Meko asked as they prepped the truck Khloe would be driving.

"She can handle herself, Mek. I'm confidant. But listen though, if anything ever happens to me, make sure you watch over her and let her take over. But have her back at all times," Samir asked of his friend.

"Nigga, what are you talking about, ain't shit gon' happen to you, my nigga. Don't even talk like that."

"I know Joe, but just promise me. I need all you niggas to promise me that y'all gon' take care of her. She's my life, bro, so I need to know that y'all got her like y'all got me,"

"I got you," Chased promised.

"So do I," Seven agreed.

"Mek, you promise, right?"

Meko sat in silence, he didn't understand where this was coming from and it began to worry him to hear Samir speak this way, but reluctantly, he agreed.

"Yea bro, I promise that Khloe would never have to worry about nothing."

Just as Meko made his promise to Samir, Cesar walked in the house as if he nothing was wrong. Instead, he decide to confront them about this so called drought because he felt it was strange that it was affecting them in Chicago, but they had work to send to Casey in Houston.

"How's everything on the home front?" Cesar asked his crew.

"Shit been desert, pussy dry out here," Meko said sarcastically.

"This shit not making no kind of sense to me at all, Joe. How we can't supply our sets, but we got work to supply Casey?" He inquired.

"Because my nigga, I made the decision to use what we got to make sure our expansion is not affected by this shit," Samir lied.

"I'm just saying, I think that's a dumb business move. We should be focusing on home instead of worried about Casey."

"First off, Ces, don't talk to me about what I should be doing and what I shouldn't be doing. Where the fuck you been at anyway? Nigga running around like he ain't apart of this family, but then wanna come in here and try to tell us what to do. Nigga, I'm the boss, not you. Always remember that," Samir snapped.

Meko quickly intervened and reminded Samir of their plan one on one. Meko had a way with Samir and he couldn't wait to snuff Cesar, but he believed in the route Samir wanted to take.

"You right boss. You're the boss," Cesar responded, sarcastically. He despised how close Samir and Meko had grown and he couldn't stomach that fact that Samir asserted his reign as leader of the Black Corleone crew.

He made up in his mind on how he was going to get the position he felt he deserved, but for now he had to get back in the good graces of his team so they would never see it coming.

After the Houston trip, things began to return back to normal. Cesar was making a conscience effort to show the rest of the Corleones the he wasn't the snake in the grass they thought he was. He began to come around in hopes that they would trust him again, so that he could put his plan in motion. He even began to fool Meko, who was the one member of the crew who always saw him for exactly who he was.

But his intense need to be the head nigga in charge wasn't about to let him stop fucking with Rocko. The more he hung out with him, the more Rocko got in his head. He convinced Cesar that they had been playing him since day one. He knew his greed would trap him and he would be an easy pawn in his ultimate goal of making the Black Corleones obsolete.

"Cesar, I heard through the grapevine this nigga Samir just made three hundred grand. Ain't y'all supposed to be in a drought, my nigga? I mean, how is that possible? I think this nigga is cutting you out of your share you deserve, plus, I don't see none of them niggas that fuck with y'all doing bad. Something just don't add up," Rocko told Cesar via Nextel chirp.

"Are you sure about that?" Cesar chirped back.

"I'm positive, my nigga, shit is mad fucked up that they fucking you over like that."

"Naw, Samir wouldn't do no shit like that."

"I'm saying, when the last time you got some bread, my nigga?"

"This nigga just gave me fifty stacks profit the other day."

"*Fifty stacks?* And this nigga just took home three hundred? Ces, don't be fooled," Rocko lied.

"Man, fuck this shit, meet me in the hood Friday, my nigga, it's time to end this shit, once and for all.

Chapter Fifteen

Samir woke up Friday morning and didn't even realize his best friend had officially turned against him. While he thought he was coming back around and seeing the errors of his ways, Cesar was plotting against his lifelong friend. He had outside niggas influencing his mind to do the unthinkable, betray his code as a Black Corleone.

Today, however, Samir couldn't focus on Cesar because he was patiently waiting for Khloe to return home from her doctor's appointment. She wasn't feeling like herself before their fight and Samir was really hoping her being so sick lately was a good indication that he had finally given a part of himself to her.

She left him a note saying she didn't want to wake him. She said his mother was taking her to her appointment. He tried his hardest not to think about the possibility of becoming a father, although he wanted nothing more in the world.

While Samir was busy pacing back and forth, Khloe was anxiously awaiting the results of her blood test. Shay was equally anxious to find out if she would be a God mother or not. Khloe's nerves were on pins and needles because although she wanted to have Samir's child, she was wondering if she was actually ready to become a mother at such a young age. Furthermore, she worried about the possibility of Samir's lifestyle finally catching up to him. As she was allowing her thoughts to control her, the doctor came in with the results.

"Well, Khloe, it looks like you're in fact, pregnant," the doctor told her.

"Oh my God, are you serious?" she asked, shocked by the news.

"Yes, I am. Based on your Hgc levels, you should be right around six weeks."

"Khloe, you're going to be a mom!" Shay said with excitement.

"Let's take a look at the baby to see if you're six weeks, why don't we," the doctor suggested.

She had Khloe lie on the table and began her ultrasound. To her amazement, she saw the little ball that was her baby. Her eyes watered as she looked at the little pitter patter of its heartbeat. She couldn't wait to tell Samir the news. Her excitement only grew when the doctor began to listen to the baby's heartbeat. Each sound of the child they created together made *her* heart beat faster.

She couldn't wait for the appointment to be over so she could get home to Samir. She knew this would lift his spirits and give his something to look forward to with everything he was going through.

After she wrapped up her appointment and the doctor gave her prenatal instructions along with her next appointment, she was excited to show Lola their first ultrasound picture.

"What did they say, dear? How did it go?" Lola asked.

"We're pregnant," Khloe smiled as she showed Lola the baby's ultrasound.

"My goodness, God is good. I am going to be a grandmother. I can't believe my baby is having a baby," she said as she hugged Khloe.

"Yea, they said I'm about six weeks along."

"I have to call Carlyle," she said as she immediately called Samir's father to tell him the news.

Carlyle's house hold was overjoyed at the thought of a new generation being born into their family. Keith and their sister Sasha were ecstatic about the arrival of their niece or nephew.

"Lyle, do not say anything to Samir. Let Khloe be the one to tell him," she insisted.

"Oh Lola, ain't nobody gon' say nothing to Samir until he calls us,"

On their way back to Khloe and Samir's suburban home, Lola notice that Khloe's excitement had dwindled and she could tell something was bothering her.

"What's wrong dear?"

"Nothing,"

"Khloe, I was born at night, not last night. Just talk to me."

"I don't know, I'm happy about the baby, but I'm not sure I want to raise a baby around Samir's lifestyle. Now that the baby is coming, I really don't know if I can handle him being out here doing what he does, but on the flip side, how do I tell him it's time to leave this life when this is who he was when I met him."

"You know Khloe, I felt the same way you're feeling right now when I found out I was pregnant with Sincere. I wanted so much for Carlyle to leave his lifestyle because of our new baby and when I found out Sincere was a boy; I wanted it even more because I didn't want to raise hustlers. I used to worry about the possibility of Carlyle not being around to raise our children due to him being caught or somebody taking his life, but sometimes we as women have to let a man be a man. But we don't have to do so lying down. When you tell Samir about the baby tell him how you feel and if he loves you the way I know he does, he'll make an effort for you," she told Khloe as they pulled up to her house.

Khloe kissed Lola and ran inside their 4,000 square feet home, screaming Samir's name. He came down from his man cave quick, thinking something was wrong with her.

"Woman, why are you screaming?"

"Because I wanted to, but anyway, you're going to be daddy in about seven and a half months," she laughed.

"Baby, don't play with me. Are you serious?"

"Yes, I'm serious. This is the first picture of your son or daughter," she handed him the ultrasound.

Samir didn't say a word; he just grabbed her and picked her up off the ground, spinning her around as he kissed her.

"I can't believe I'm about to be a father. This is the best thing anybody has ever given me."

Samir immediately called his boys to let them know the news of Khloe's pregnancy and to make sure they would all meet them at Lawry's the next day because he decided right then that this was as good a moment as any to finally ask her to marry him. That day was one of the best days of his life and things couldn't get any better, or so he thought.

While Samir was basking in the excitement of having a child to carry his name, Cesar was meeting up with Rocko and the Oglesby Boys on how he wanted to move, regarding his position as a Corleone. He had allowed Rocko to pollute his mind so much toward his own crew that he was ready to dismantle the movement that he had helped put together.

Cesar wanted to be the man by any means necessary and he couldn't do that with Samir in the way, always throwing his position in his face. And what's worse, he hated feeling like he had to get permission to move how he wanted to move within his own territory.

Rocko had succeeded in his plan to use Cesar as his pawn. He had officially lit the match that would burn the Black Corleone foundation to the ground.

"You sure this how you wanna go about it?" Rocko pretended like he was concerned about the plan Cesar put forth.

"Nigga, does a bitch's pussy bleed?" Cesar snapped.

"After that, then what do we do next?"

"We go take what's mine. That means work,

money, everything. This shit all belongs to me. I'm the fucking man. Wouldn't be no fucking Black Corleones if it wasn't for me, fuck love. The only thing Cesar is loyal to is Cesar. It's time the city finally give me my fucking respect, and it's about time niggas is saying Cesar's name. Samir's problem and the rest of them niggas problem is they too worried about love when niggas should have been worried about money. Fuck love, I'm loyal to my fucking money."

"Alright nigga, damn... calm down. Once this shit is done it ain't no turning back," Rocko smiled knowing he was just one step closer to his ultimate goal.

Cesar's greed blinded him to the fact that the love he thought he was getting from Rocko was just a game to get him to do the dirty work. His greed and need for respect that he didn't earn was about to lead him down a path of destruction.

Chapter Sixteen

The sun peaked through Samir's Italian curtains, waking him up from a deep slumber. For some strange reason he didn't feel like himself. He pondered on how his life would be if he had chosen a different route. He didn't know why he was starting to think about changing the way he moved. Maybe it was the fact that he was about to become a father. *Is this the life he wanted for his son? Is this the example he wanted to teach his child?*

He glanced at Khloe as she slept and fell deeper in love with her knowing that growing inside her was a piece of him. He leaned over and placed his head on her womb as if he was hoping to hear his child speak to him.

"I don't know if you can hear me, but it's me, daddy. I just want you to know that I love you with everything in me. I know I haven't always made the best decisions in life, but I promise I'm gonna make sure you never want for anything. I promise you that daddy won't let nothing hurt you and I promise you that I won't spend your whole life in this game. I don't want you to be like me, I want you to be better than me. I promise you that today your daddy is going to start making the transition out of this game so that you don't grow up wanting to aspire to be a hustler. I hope you know that you and your mommy are the best thing that ever happened to me," he finished his speech with a kiss to Khloe's stomach.

"Do your really mean that, Samir?" Khloe asked him as she snuggled under his arm.

"Do I really mean what?"

"Do you really mean that one day you are going to walk away from this life?"

"Yes baby, I really mean it. I promise you and our child that I'm gonna get out very soon. Khloe, do you know how much I love you?"

"Yes, I know Samir."

"Naw, like do you really; from the bottom of your heart know how much I love you? I only wanted to make you happy. I hope I've made you happy since we been together."

"I know you love me, Samir. I love you too, and you've made me the happiest girl in the world, I can't wait to have your baby."

"I was gonna wait 'til tonight to ask you this, but I need to know now. Will you be my wife?" he asked, as he pulled the 5 carat Tiffany diamond ring out of his bed side table.

"Samir, wait... is this a joke?" She asked; her eyes wide.

"No, Khloe, this is not a joke."

"Oh my God, baby, yeeesss... of course I'll marry you," she said as he placed the ring on her finger.

"This has to be a dream baby. I can't believe all this is happening to me."

"I only wanna make you happy."

They consummated their engagement twice before Samir sent her shopping for their dinner that night. He decided he had to go see his brothers and tell them about his baby and his engagement. While he got dressed he thought about his life and he could see every scene of the last four and half years play out like a movie. He thought about how different his life would be if he walked away from a game he so desperately wanted to be in. But his unborn child was worth him leaving all this behind. Khloe and that baby meant more to him than the money he made or the name he built. He knew it would take time, but he was now focused on the promise he made his unborn baby.

Music Playing

Feel me now, Listen, Momma love me, Pop left, Mickey fed me, Annie dressed me, Eric fought me, made me tougher, love you for that my nigga, no matter what bruh, Marcy raised me, and whether right or wrong, streets gave me all I write in this song.

As the slow tempo of Momma Loves Me from *Jay Z*'s new Blueprint album blared through his Escalade speakers, Samir's life continued to play in his mind. He didn't know where the sudden change came from, but today didn't feel like a regular day to him. He never thought about his life this much. He didn't know if he could walk away from the empire he built. He was Samir Corleone and he worried he could never really get away from the reputation he built in the streets. *Even when he did decide to walk away from this life, could he ever live like every normal functioning person in society?*

All he had known his entire life was the game and now he was wondering why he jumped in it in the first place. His situation with Cesar was starting to weigh on him too. He never thought in a million years Cesar would turn on him the way he did. He believed in Cesar even when nobody else did.

As the music continued to play, Samir shed a tear for the first time in his life. He was gaining a new life in his child, but losing his brother. Before he realized it, he had arrived in the parking lot of the county jail. He sat there a while and gathered his thoughts as the music continued to play.

Money pouring in, clientele growing now, birth of my first nephew, time to slow it down, Oct twenty first Lavell came in the world, followed by three more boys, then a baby girl, momma loves me, te-te, uncle jay loves you to death, won't let no trouble come your way.

As the tracked continued to play on repeat, Samir couldn't help but to think about his unborn child and how different he wanted his life to be. He was excited to tell his brothers about him becoming a father, but he didn't know if he should tell them that he was ready to transition out with them being so close to their release. He knew Ace and Sin would want to continue the reign with him, but his child made all that seem trivial.

After going through the normal visitation procedure, Samir was once again face to face with his older brothers. He had spent his entire dope boy life without them and he was excited that they wouldn't miss Khloe's pregnancy and the birth of his child.

"What's up Samir," Ace greeted.

"We weren't expecting you 'till next week, bro," Sin also greeted him.

"I know, I just really needed to see you guys," Samir told them.

"Oh, okay, well, what's going on? You don't seem like yourself today," Sin asked him.

"Nothing bro, I'm good. I just wanted to come down here and see my brothers for a second. It ain't nothing wrong with that, is it?"

"No, ain't no issues with that at all," Ace told him.

"Honestly though bro, I want y'all to know how much I looked up to the both of you. I spent my whole life wanting to be like my big brothers. Hell, y'all been my driving force behind this Corleone shit. Everything I've done, I've done because I wanted to impress the two of you. I just wanted y'all to be proud of me."

"Samir, we are proud of you. We couldn't have asked for a better baby brother. I mean, shit, you did shit we only dreamed of. I'm sorry we weren't around for you during this time but I swear when we get out it's us against the world," Sin told him.

"Well, I'm about to do one more thing y'all haven't done."

"What's that?" Ace asked.

"I'm about to have a baby. Khloe found out she was pregnant yesterday."

"No shit, Samir," Sin said with a huge smile on his face.

"Yea, she's about six weeks," he said as he showed them the ultrasound of his baby.

"Damn Samir, I don't know what to say but congratulations. I'm about to be a uncle," Ace said in excitement.

Samir and his brothers spent the rest of his visit talking about the next phase of Samir's life and before he left he made sure he told them how much he loved them.

On the way out he called his mother, but she didn't answer, so he left her a message. He apologized for the choices he made and told her no matter what, he could have never done any of this without her support. After the message for his mother, he sent his father a message via his two-way.

I love you too son. I've always been proud of you and the man you became. I hope your son makes you half as proud as you've made me. I'll see you and your girl tomorrow at the house for family dinner.

Chapter Seventeen

When Samir arrived home later that evening, Khloe was already getting dressed for their dinner. She was standing in the bathroom of their master suite in a pink Victoria secret bra and panty set, putting ear rings in her ears.

Samir walked up behind her and kissed her neck. He held on to her with one hand on her belly as he looked at the two of them in the mirror. He felt blessed that he had her in his life. He felt that she deserved more than a drug dealer to call her husband. In fact, she could have easily found some college football star or a medical student, but she chose him.

He held onto her for dear life and thought about how much he wanted to change for her and their baby. She began to get nervous by his actions that day but she didn't say a word, she just watched as he jumped in the shower.

"Samir, I love you, okay," she said on the other

side of shower door.

"I love you too, Khloe. I swear I love you more than life itself."

They didn't say much after that. They got dressed and headed out the door when Samir got a call from Cesar.

"What's up, Joe?" Cesar said through Samir's Nextel.

"Ain't shit, what's up? You headed downtown to the spot or what?"

"That's what I called to tell you. I'm not gon' be able to make it to the dinner because I'm 'bout to hit this road with my cousins on a little vacation down to Miami," Cesar told him.

"Come on bro, it's my engagement dinner."

"I know Joe, I feel bad as hell, but we driving and that's a long trip. But look though, I wanted to make sure I give you this money before I leave."

"I'm on my way to dinner bro and we already late, just wait till you get back."

"SC, you already know how I am when I get around pretty bitches with fat asses. I don't wanna fuck off this bread. I need to square this away."

"Aight, fuck it, where you at?"

"I'm in Harvey right now."

"Okay, just meet me at Arnies."

Samir hung up the phone and looked at Khloe

who was obviously irritated. Samir would have never taken care of business during a time that was dedicated to her.

"This is only gonna take a minute Khloe, I promise,"

"Samir, why can't you do that shit tomorrow, it's our engagement dinner and everybody is already waiting for us."

"I know baby. Just let me handle this and we will be on our way, I swear."

"Whatever Samir," Khloe was upset.

Samir smiled because now that she was pregnant her bratty ways made her beautiful in his eyes and he could use her hormones as an excuse.

They sat in front of Arnies for what seemed like ten minutes when a blue Tahoe pulled up alongside them. Khloe decided to go inside for ice cream while he handled his business with Cesar, but before she got out the care he grabbed her hand and kissed her on her cheek.

"What was that for?" she asked him

"Nothing, I just love you, beautiful," he told her, flashing the smile she fell in love with the very first time she saw him in Harolds. She didn't say a word; she just smiled back and went inside.

Samir watched Khloe walk inside the restaurant before he got out of his truck. Khloe watched what was transpiring as she waited in line to order. She watched Samir get out of his truck and before she could realize what was happening she heard the loud pop of the first gunshot and she felt a the customer in front of her pull her down to the ground to shield her from harm.

Her heart beat faster as she fought for him to let her go. She screamed Samir's name over and over as she heard pop after pop after pop, followed by the sound of tires burning rubber as the Tahoe sped off.

When the smoke cleared, the witness finally let her go and she ran outside, praying Samir was safe, but when she made it outside, Samir was slumped against their truck, gasping for air. Before she could think, she was holding onto him trying to stop the bleeding.

"Samir, baby, please, baby, just breath... baby breath," she cried as he looked in her eyes. "Just breath, baby..."

"Ma'am is he okay?' a stranger asked.

"No, he's been shot, please help me!" she cried as he held onto him tighter, "Samir, baby please, just hold on okay. Please."

"The ambulance is on the way. Just keep talking to him."

Khloe held onto Samir for dear life as the crowd

increased around her. She could hear the sounds of sirens speeding toward her location. Samir never took his eyes off of her. Tears streamed down his face and it was becoming harder for him to breath. She grabbed his hand and felt him grip it for dear life.

"Just hold on, Samir, baby, the ambulance is here. Just hold on."

The paramedics frantically rushed to Samir and Khloe's location as the police tried to keep the crowd back.

"Ma'am, are you okay?" a paramedic asked, as they placed oxygen on Samir's face and began go cut his clothes, so they could get a better look at his wounds. They got him onto the gurney and rushed him to the ambulance with Khloe never leaving his side.

"Ma'am, I think it's best if you ride with me," a plain clothed officer said as he tried to pull Khloe away from the gurney.

"No, hell no! I wanna ride with Samir. He needs to know that I'm next to him. He needs to see me. We just found out we were going to have a baby yesterday and today he asked me to marry him. Did you know that? We were on our way to our engagement dinner. He needs to know that his baby and his wife are next to him," she cried to the officer.

Feeling sorry for her, he helped her into the back of the ambulance. She couldn't get to him with the paramedics around him, so she told them to tell him she was there.

"Samir, Can you hear me? You've been shot and we are taking you to Ingalls hospital. I need you to stay with me. We're almost there. And Khloe and your baby is here, she is right here with you, okay," the paramedic said loudly, granting Khloe's request.

On the ride to the hospital she felt her purse vibrate. She looked at her phone and saw Meko's number on her caller ID.

"Meko," she could barely answer through her tears.

"Khloe, what's wrong, why are you crying and what is all that noise?" Meko said frantically on the other end of the phone.

"They shot him, Meko, they shot him..."

"Khloe, what the fuck are you talking about? They shot who? little sis, talk to me, who shot who?"

"Samir! They shot Samir, Meko!"

The Black Corleones
3
COMING SOON!